# BECOMING FIRE

## Experience the Presence of Jesus Every Day

We know, even in ordinary life, how it occasionally happens that, when a person constantly associates with another individual living on a higher level than he himself has hitherto done, how gradually and insensibly he is lifted up above himself, and becomes like to him whose whole conversation he so justly admires; so that in a few years a remarkable improvement of character takes place. And so, only in a greater degree, is it with those earnest souls who live much with Jesus; having His life constantly before them, daily and hourly learning from Him. By more intimate acquaintance with Christ, they are not only drawn nearer to Him, but are drawn to love Him more deeply, to trust in Him more entirely and become more like Him in their daily living.

—Thomas à Kempis
Meditations on the Life of Christ

# BECOMING FIRE

*Experience the Presence
of Jesus Every Day*

*Jeanie Miley*

PEAKE ROAD
Macon, Georgia

ISBN 1-57312-193-2

*Becoming Fire*
*Experience the Presence of Jesus Every Day*

Jeanie Miley

Copyright © 1998
Peake Road
Smyth & Helwys Publishing, Inc.
6316 Peake Road
Macon, Georgia 31210-3960
1-800-747-3016

The paper used in this publication meets the
minimum requirements of American National Standard
for Information Sciences—Permanence of Paper for
Printed Library Materials, ANSI Z39.48–1984.

*Library of Congress Cataloguing-in-Publication Data*
Miley, Jeanie.
    Becoming fire: experience the presence of
    Jesus every day / Jeanie Miley.
    p.      cm.
    Originally published: Grand Rapids, Mich.:
    F. A. Revell, © 1993.
    ISBN 1-57312-193-2 (alk. paper)
    1. Jesus Christ—Presence—Meditations.
    2. Bible. N.T. Gospels—Mediations. I. Title.
    [BT590.P75M454      1998]
    242'.2—dc21                                    98-17457
                                                      CIP

To my father,
Louis Daniel Ball,
whose passion for Christ changed his story and mine,
and enflamed my mind, my heart, and my imagination
with a love that will not let me go

# Contents

# Foreword

I can still see my grandmother sitting in her favorite chair in the living room putting her ear as close to the radio as possible. She was often listening to her favorite afternoon soap opera. Saturday morning was our time to listen. There was our favorite program of "Let's Pretend," which featured a special fairy tale each week and was introduced by a melody that still rings in my ears.

This was followed by "The Lincoln Highway," a series of stories that took place on U.S. 30, which happened to pass right though the state of Indiana where I lived. I also re-member that after school I would rush home to get the latest episode of "Jack Armstrong, the All-American Boy."

Radio was a cool medium that required a very active imagination on the part of the listener. As TV began to become popular, it was called a hot medium that required less and less of our own creativity. I remember when the "Lone Ranger" appeared on television, I was disgusted to note that the picture was not nearly as attractive and excit-ing as the one in my imagination. It was the same thing with the pictures in the Bible storybooks. They were very color-ful and exciting, but not nearly up to the quality of my own imaginings as I heard the stories read to me.

What Jeanie Miley has done for me in this book is to call me back to a fruitful use of my creative imagination that I seemed to have lost with the coming of television and my continued schooling. She has led me to ask the Holy Spirit again to bring fire and light to this great mental capability we have in our imaginations. It makes sense that if we are to touch the Holy Spirit of God in our present moment, it has to be done with the "hands" of our imagination and a heart that is willing to stretch itself or discipline itself to listen at a deep level.

In this book, she leads us from activating our imagination to experiencing a deeper contemplation. Is what Jeanie Miley does for us in this book something new? No. It is as old as the Bible itself.

A thousand years before the Scriptures were ever written down, they were shared around the campfires of a nomadic people. The Bible as we know it today is really a library of stories, poems, and songs that were collected from these fireside experiences. Even after the stories were put on scrolls, the Jewish people invented a literary form called "midrash." It was a meditation on the sacred text or an imaginative reconstruction of the scene or episode narrated. Its goal was always the practical application to the present, so Bible stories were told in such a way to give new light and direction to the people who read them.

You can see that what Jeanie Miley is doing in this book is very similar to a Jewish literary form that is more that 2,500 years old. An example of this is found in the New Testament Acts of the Apostles 7:22-32. When compared with Exodus 2:11-15, you begin to see the influence of the midrash writers.

When it comes to the New Testament, the stories and parables of Jesus were written, not so much to give us theological insights, but to take us in wonder to the Father. Holy men and women throughout the Christian era have called us to keep our imaginations open to the Spirit of God. St. Francis, the poor person's spiritual director, worked to invent the crib scene one Christmas Eve to touch these people at a deeper spiritual level. Francis likewise created the stations of the cross, so people could better imagine what it was like to make that journey from Pilate's court to Golgotha's hill. Ignatius Loyola, a layman of the sixteenth century, discovered in a long retreat that by using all of the senses one was better able to understand the mystery of the

Scriptures. It was his active imagination exercises that led Teresa of Avila to always depend on an image of Jesus to lead her to prayer. On the other hand, her spiritual director, John of the Cross, who likewise became a great contemplative, seemed never to depend upon these images.

Storytellers of all ages have challenged us to use our holy imaginations to come closer to our invisible God, or to overcome the obstacles that separate us from our brothers and sisters. Jeanie Milcy belongs to this tradition. I, for one, am very much indebted to her work. At a retreat, I gave each person one of these seven meditations on the Transfiguration and asked them to follow the process she outlines in her introduction: read the Scripture, use her meditation and question, spend twenty minutes of taking it deep inside yourself. As they began to share their experiences with each other, there was great enthusiasm over how God was revealed to each of them. On a five-day directed retreat, I asked the retreatants to stop seven times during the day using her prayer and meditation format. After a day or so, the retreatants were able to create their own meditations in a way similar to Jeanie's.

The gift of imagination was not used much by us after we left school. Then movies and TV did a lot of the work for us. So we must be patient with ourselves as we practice this process. My guess is that you may have to spend seven weeks of seven days before it becomes your own. If this does not bring you to prayer, you have lost nothing except time. But if, as a result, you come to a new dimension of deep contemplative prayer, then you are the one for whom this book was written.

—Fr. Keith Hosey
Diocesan Priest, Hartford City, Indiana
Director, John XXIII Retreat Center

# *Introduction*

What does it mean to "know Jesus"? How can we walk and talk with someone who lived nearly two thousand years ago? Can the dynamic, vibrant love of Jesus move out of history and into the everyday concerns of modern life?

For this Western-trained, pragmatic mind, a vital, personal love relationship with the Son of God seems mystical and ethereal. I need something I can put my hands on! I believe something when I see it. In the spiritual life, however, there are moments when I am touched by a power I cannot explain, or I burn with that consuming fire of a love that will not let me go. It is when the Living Christ grasps me that I am able to believe, and then I see. The evidences of the Living Christ appear in the most common, ordinary, everyday events.

Many believers study the teachings of Christ, know the facts about his life and death, his resurrection and ascension, but may not know how to incorporate the power of that life in daily living. There are sincere and committed Christian who worship a faraway God who is over all things, but they do not understand the God who is near and present in all things.

To imprison Jesus Christ back in history is to miss the power and presence of the Living Christ who is with us even now. To relate to him solely as a faraway God deprives the believer of the immanent Friend who walks alongside, longing to give power and love, grace and joy to those of us who are trying to make it on our own.

Through the power of the Holy Spirit, God can use our imagination to bring the person of Jesus Christ near. By meditating on the encounters Jesus had with people in the days he walked on the earth as a human being, it is possible for us to be touched and changed by him even as those people were.

When Jesus was on earth, he walked right into the middle of the human condition and got all mixed up with human need. He reached out to all kinds of individuals, discerning their deepest needs and confronting their barriers. He called the unlearned and untrained to become disciplined followers. He had good times with his friends and broke bread with them.

While he was a citizen of this world, Jesus healed the sick, exorcised evil, and restored life, physical and spiritual. In all his encounters, Jesus Christ lifted individuals up toward wholeness, transforming them with the holy fire of his presence. I believe he longs to do the same with contemporary followers as they make themselves available through particular disciplines, one of which is practicing the presence of Christ. Becoming Fire is a manual to aid the practice of the Living Presence.

On a warm summer evening, I sat down with Clay Ries, a friend from a religious tradition much different from mine. As we explored the different ways people meet Christ, he shared with me some of the spiritual disciplines of his heritage that had empowered his own personal life.

As we talked about the differences between the observance of the Lord's Supper in my tradition and the celebration of the Eucharist in his tradition, Clay told me about his understanding of the Living Presence of Christ. And then he said something that captured my imagination and fired my heart with new questions and new understanding. "It does not make sense to me that just because I didn't live two thousand years ago, I cannot have the experience of being with Christ."

That idea had never entered my mind! Clay's comment haunted me through the months of preparation for writing this book. The more I worked with these encounters with Jesus, the more I realized that through the power of the Holy Spirit at work in the powerful gift of imagination, God has made it possible for us to be with Jesus in a new way. The most revolutionary discovery for my own life was the revelation that while I may think I am choosing to be with Christ, there is never a time when the Living Christ is not with me.

While I cannot have the exact experiences the disciples had, the Living Christ adapts himself to the point of my own need. By meditating on the stories in the Gospels, by identifying with the characters, by using the physical senses, I can draw close to the one who has already drawn close to me.

By using these encounters with Jesus as the seeds for meditation, we may hear Jesus himself speaking to our deepest needs, the same basic needs he met in the people of his day. By mulling the stories over and over in our minds, we let the truths of the stories sift down into our hearts and produce change. By getting acquainted with Jesus through the active use of imagination, our minds are renewed, and we are transformed. This method of prayer is a way of praying the Scriptures.

In using the meditations in this book, you may start at the beginning, or you may wish to scan the encounters and see which one chooses you; in other words, let your need lead you to the encounter that will be meaningful to you.

It is best to devote a period of time each day to the meditations, using only one each day. Read the story in the Scripture, read the meditation, and then close your eyes and experience the encounter. Allow the Holy Spirit at least twenty minutes to work, using your imagination to play the scene over and over. Then, sit quietly with an open mind and a listening heart and just "be with" the story.

It is important to read the Scripture each day. If the event is related in another one of the Gospels, read it as well. Throughout the week, mull over the passage as you go about your ordinary routine. Consciously call it to mind and pray a prayer of openness, placing yourself in a receptive mind-set to the Spirit of Christ. Recreate the physical scene as often as you can, always seeing yourself there. Carry this scene in your imagination.

God's Spirit seems to present truths to us when we relax. Rather than demanding an insight, simply wait; you cannot control when God will reveal God's self and the truth God wants you to gain. But God will honor your asking, seeking, and knocking. God may speak to you at the very time you are involved in meditating on the passage. More likely, God may reveal the truth from the Gospel story while you are going about your daily activities. The insight may pop into your head as you are driving in a car pool or repairing an office machine. The key is in maintaining an attitude of expectancy.

Using a journal to record your responses to the questions in the daily meditations is a powerful way to retain the insights and guidance you receive. While it is not necessary to have the same time and same place every day for this experience, it does seem helpful to be consistent. God honors our diligence, and the benefits of working with these meditations is cumulative.

In beginning any kind of spiritual growth process, it is important to relinquish your own preconceived expectations of what should happen. Let Christ's Spirit be in charge of this process. Let him lead you where he wants you to go, reveal to you the insights he wants you to have, and do with you what he wills. One thing is assured: you will be changed!

As the spark of Christ's love is ignited in your heart, allow time, receptiveness, and continual prayer to fan the flame, burning away the dross and bringing from the fire the person God wants you to be. Out of the refining fire, you will be transformed; you will become his light in the world.

An old tale from the desert fathers related by George Maloney in his book Why Not Become Totally Fire? tells of a disciple who went to Abba Joseph and said, "Father, according to my strength I sing a few psalms, I pray and fast a little, I meditate, and as well as I can I cleanse my thoughts. Now what more can I do?" Abba Joseph stood up, spreading his hands toward heaven. His fingers were like ten lamps of fire. "If you want," Abba Joseph said, "why not become totally fire?"

Encountering Jesus through the stories of the Gospels is a way of becoming fire.

# What Do You Want?

JOHN 1:35-39

# Day 1

In your imagination, see yourself standing in the center of a small village. You are leaning against the wall of a shop in the marketplace, chatting with friends.

Visualize in your mind's eye the blue sky overhead and the dusty street. Watch the people passing in front of you. See a young mother with her baby strapped to her body; she is smiling and talking with a group of women at the well across the street. You watch a group of children running back and forth between the buildings.

Hear an old man, dressed in the garb of a rabbi, calling to a friend. Listen to a stooped beggar woman working the crowd, pleading for alms. The song of a bird on a nearby ledge catches your attention even as a slight breeze stirs the air.

Your friends are discussing a topic that is terribly important, and you would enter into the discussion with enthusiasm, except that a man across the street rivets your attention and you lose interest in what your friends are saying. There is something so compelling about him that you can't take your eyes away from him.

"That is Jesus," your friend John says.

*What do you see in Jesus*
*that catches your attention today?*

# Day 2

Return in your imagination to the setting of yesterday. Jesus, the carpenter from Nazareth, has caught your attention.

What is so compelling about Jesus that you want to meet him? Is it the way he approaches the people in the village, giving dignity and respect to everyone he encounters? Is it the way he looks at people and the way he touches them with compassion that draws you to him? Could it be his look of tenderness and love that captures your heart?

Your teacher and friend, John, notices that you are captivated by Jesus. Whereas your attention has been focused on John's teachings, now you are drawn to someone else.

"That is Jesus, the Lamb of God," you hear John say, and suddenly your attention is pulled back to the man beside you. John knows that you will leave him now, and you feel the pain of separation. You look down because you don't know what to say. All kinds of feelings flood your heart. As you look up into John's eyes, you realize that he is letting you go. He who could hold on to you is giving you permission to follow another teacher, and to sit at the feet of someone else.

"This is the way it is supposed to be," he tells you. "My job was to prepare the way for you to be with him."

*What good things do you need to surrender
in order to follow Jesus?*

3

# *Day 3*

Suddenly, there in the busy marketplace, you are following Jesus. You feel the press of the crowd against you as you weave your way among the men and women. You almost trip over a child who darts out in front of you, and for a moment you lose sight of Jesus.

You step up your pace to find him and notice that he has stopped to visit with a vendor. You slow down and watch him purchase a piece of fruit. You are vaguely aware that your friend, another student of John, is behind you, but you don't talk with him. Your attention is fixed on Jesus.

In your imagination, notice how Jesus walks with ease and grace among the people. He seems to be well-known, and you can tell by his friendliness that he likes people and that they like him.

Suddenly, Jesus turns to you and looks straight into your face. You catch your breath and, for a moment, consider turning away. You may be getting in over your head.

Imagine that you move closer to Jesus until you are standing face to face with him. You know, although you don't know how you know, that this is a turning point and that you will never be the same.

*What is it like for Jesus to look at you?*

*What do you do when he gazes into your eyes?*

# Day 4

"What do you want?" Jesus asks you. It is such a simple question, and yet you know that how you answer that question is going to shape the rest of your days.

"I saw you following me," Jesus says. You turn to your friend as a slight blush washes across your face. Then you look back to Jesus. His compelling force is so great that you don't concern yourself with being embarrassed.

Standing there, poised between your old life and the future, you feel alive as never before. Time seems to stand still. All the colors around you are vivid; the sounds are clear and almost musical.

What do you say when Jesus asks what you want? Do you even know what you want? As you stand there, enclosed in a holy space even in the midst of a crowd, you examine your heart.

Are you coming to Jesus out of curiosity? Do you have some need you think he might meet or an intellectual question he might answer? Is there something in you that needs to be healed? Is there some brokenness, a piercing or unrelenting pain, a failure from your past that you would like him to carry? Do you need forgiveness? Are you dying for love? Is there something you have tried to fix that escapes your skill?

*Exactly what do you want from Jesus of Nazareth?*

*Tell him,*
*in your prayer of the heart,*
*exactly what you need.*

# *Day 5*

In your imagination, recall a time when you were put on the spot and needed to answer a question but couldn't. Remember how your mind whirled and offered up a jumble of nonsense when you needed to be clear and direct with your response. Is this the way you might be with Jesus, standing in the marketplace with him? Do you know what you would like from him?

Perhaps this is one of those times when your mind works perfectly and you are completely calm and centered. You know exactly what you want from Jesus, and you are articulate and concise with your request. How does it feel to ask him directly for what you need?

Still another response to Jesus' question, "What do you want?" might be to turn your attention away from the thoughts tumbling over and over in your mind. Imagine that you are so captivated by his presence that you turn your focus to him, putting aside your cares and concerns for the time being. Hear yourself asking him where he lives.

*How can you ask*
*such a personal question of Jesus?*

*Aren't you risking rejection*
*by such a presumptuous inquiry?*

*How does he look at you*
*when you seek to invade his privacy?*

*Do you really want to know where Jesus is staying?*

*Are you sure you want to get that close to pure holiness?*

6

# Day 6

Suddenly, you become aware of the boldness in your question, but before you can turn away in embarrassment, Jesus reaches out and touches your arm.

"Come and see," he tells you, and in that invitation, he opens up his life for your scrutiny and involvement.

You follow along behind him, thinking of all that you have heard about him and all that you would like to ask him. You wonder where he is taking you, but you no longer want to turn away. It isn't simple curiosity that beckons you down the narrow pathway. There is something in you that so much wants to know what this man Jesus has, or who he is, that you are willing to leave your daily responsibilities and follow him wherever he goes.

There is a hospitality about Jesus that makes you feel at ease and at home. He is interested in who you are and what you do with your days and weeks. He wants to know about you, but he also tells you about himself.

What is that feeling you have in response to Jesus' transparency? He is so at home with himself that you feel at home with yourself. Because there is no competitiveness in Jesus, you feel safe and free to speak out of your heart. He doesn't judge you. He doesn't interrupt. He listens intently to every word.

*How do you feel about being friends with Jesus?*

# Day 7

It is late in the day, and you become aware that you have spent the day with Jesus. When you get up and tell him goodbye, he asks you to come back.

On the dusty path home in the late afternoon, your mind goes over the things Jesus said. You have never seen a rabbi make himself so vulnerable to his students, and your mind is trying to process the depth of this man. There is something different about him, and you feel different after being with him.

As Jesus made himself known to you, you learned new things about yourself. You see possibilities that weren't there before you spent time with him. You sense that there is more to life with him than you ever dreamed, and you find yourself thinking about how you can rearrange your schedule to spend more time with him.

Instead of going home, you walk out into the countryside and find a large rock to sit on. You stay there a long time, thinking back over your time with Jesus.

All the things you thought you wanted or needed—security, power, position, authority—have faded in importance. The things that seemed so dark and hopeless now seem manageable.

*How will you arrange to spend more time with Jesus?*

# What Do You Have to Lose?

Luke 18:18-30

# *Day 1*

Using your imagination, see yourself as a person who has position and power in your community. Take a minute to list your assets; feel the satisfaction of all you have accomplished in your lifetime.

You have lived by a certain set of standards and rules. Where did you get those standards? Do you take pride in keeping the rules?

You have heard about Jesus of Nazareth and his teachings, and have been trying to decide how to incorporate his message into your rules and into the religious traditions you have followed all your life. You have heard him speak of eternal life, and you want to know how to have that.

As you sit in the silence, ponder the meaning of eternal life. Is your concept of eternal life simply living on and on? Or is it a quality of life that begins now in relationship with Christ?

Moving back in time, see yourself in the marketplace of a village walking up to Jesus. How does it feel for you to approach him? Are you hesitant or bold?

See Jesus turn to you. Hear yourself asking him what you would have to do to have this eternal life.

*Are you seeking Jesus*
*because you are looking for eternal life,*
*or because you want a Band-Aid for your problems?*

# Day 2

Jesus knew "what was in a man," and so he was able to see the true question and the real need of the young man in the Scripture. He could tell by his bearing that he was a member of the ruling class; perhaps Jesus even knew something about the man's background. Jesus met the man where he was, by stating for him what he already knew.

Imagine that it's you standing before Jesus. You are talking to him, trying to flatter him by calling him "good." Are you seeking to "win points" with him? Then you realize that as he looks at you, he knows everything about you, just as he knew everything about the young man. He knows what is in your heart, and he hears the real questions beneath the ones you verbalize.

Hear the love and understanding in Jesus' voice even as he reminds you that only God is good. Become aware that Jesus sees through your words and deeds to your real motivation. Are you meticulous about keeping certain rules? Do you go through the motions of your worship without noticing any change in your life?

*How does it feel to be fully known by Jesus?*
*Do you want to run away?*
*Or do you feel fully accepted and loved?*

*Verbalize your deepest need to Jesus.*
*Listen for his response.*
*Does he care about your need?*
*Will he meet it?*

## Day 3

The rich young ruler was sincere about his question to Jesus. He seemed to have been a "good enough" man—he had kept the laws as he understood them, but something was missing. He had done all of the external things that were supposed to bring him happiness. Yet, he still felt a need to seek out Jesus for the answer to his yearning for something more.

What are the things you have looked to in your life to give you meaning and purpose?

| | |
|---|---|
| good deeds | family |
| financial security | things |
| church activities | pleasure |
| position and power | success |
| following the rules | education |

As you stand before Jesus, as the rich young ruler did, become aware of your feeling of neediness. No matter how hard you have tried or how much you have accomplished or acquired, nothing fills that deep inner yearning of your heart.

It isn't that those things that have filled your life aren't good or valuable. Rather, when you come into the presence of Jesus, you realize they don't seem very important.

*What would it take for you to know
the joy of your salvation?*

*What would it take for you to be truly happy?*

*Do you believe Jesus can fill your neediness?*

# Day 4

Imagine that you have just asked Jesus of Nazareth to tell you the secret of eternal life, and he has said that you must be willing to let go of all the things you hold dear in order to gain eternal life.

Your mind flips rapidly through the things that are important to you. You feel your heart beating more rapidly as you think about giving them up. You don't know how it would feel to let go of your dependence on family or work. You can't imagine life without your ceaseless striving to be good enough, rich or smart enough, pretty or strong enough.

What is your reaction to Jesus telling you that you must give up everything and follow him? What does he mean by "giving it up"?

In your imagination, do you turn away from Jesus? Do you try to negotiate with him? Do you argue with him or ignore what he says? Do you tell him why what he has suggested isn't practical?

*How does Jesus look at you as you explain why*
*you can't possibly give up what he has asked you to give up?*

*In "real life," how do you try*
*to squirm out of this hard requirement of Jesus?*

*What would happen if you were willing*
*to surrender completely to him?*

*What do you have to lose if you make this surrender?*

*What would you gain?*

*Day 5*

As you stand before Jesus, picture how he is looking at you as he waits for you to search your mind and heart and come up with a decision about what you will do with him.

Recall a time when you got in over your head. Remember the feeling of getting involved before you knew what would be asked of you. This time you are cautious, and yet you know the direction you must go and the decision you must make if you are to find true meaning, purpose, and joy in life.

You tell yourself that, after all, you are the one who approached Jesus with your question about eternal life. You are the one who sought him out. Feel the tension building in your entire body as Jesus waits for your answer.

As you look into the face of Jesus, what is his expression as he waits for your answer? What does he do? How do you think he feels about your exerting your free will to live in bondage to people, places, and things?

Jesus offers a quality of life that is higher and greater than any person or thing can offer. He offers an abundance of love, joy, and peace. His spirit is always at work, empowering his followers to live in the wider place of his freedom and grace. He wants a victorious life for you.

*Are you ready for Jesus to do all he can do for you?*

*Day 6*

Imagine that you are one of the disciples witnessing the young seeker's encounter with Jesus. You stand a few feet away, and you can hear their conversation and watch the expressions on their faces. Do you identify with the young man's struggle? What do you learn about how to relate to seekers by watching Jesus with this young man?

Think about all you have given up to follow Christ. Think about all you have gained because you have made him the first of your priorities.

How do you feel as Jesus explains the requirement for eternal life to the man who wanted an easier answer? Do you feel self-righteous or regretful? Do you feel anger or anguish for him as he battles out his decision? Do you feel frustration or pity? Would you behave harshly or gently with him?

If you are asked to walk alongside someone who is in the process of yielding his life to Christ, what do you do to support and encourage him? Is there anything you do that might discourage him or her?

*Is Christ asking you to be*
*a messenger of encouragement to someone today?*

# *Day 7*

Jesus moved confidently into the lives of the people he touched, and turned their priorities upside down. He insisted that they put him first in their affections.

Jesus knew that all of the good things of our lives could become idols to us, keeping us from surrender to him. He also knew that because of our bent toward willfulness, we might choose idols of destruction, habits and substances that could defeat us. He knew that we would allow others to be first in our affections and that we would let them set our priorities and determine how we spend our time, money, and giftedness.

In your imagination, stand before Christ and tell him how well those other idols in your life are really doing at giving you happiness. Tell him all the people who might be inconvenienced if you chose to put him first in your affections. Hear Jesus' gentle but firm voice telling you that whatever is in first place in your life will destroy you, or you will destroy it.

See Jesus look straight through your defenses and ask you to name whatever is keeping you from an unhindered love relationship with him. Hear him ask you what is holding you back from complete surrender to him.

*Are you ready to release your life into Jesus' hands?*

*Hear yourself telling Jesus*
*that you will give him your first affection.*

*What is his response to you?*

# Water into Wine

JOHN 2:1-11

*Day 1*

*You are cordially invited*
*To share the joy of*
*A wedding celebration in Cana*

Pretend that you are part of the community of Cana in Galilee at the time of Jesus. What will you wear to the wedding? What gift will you take for the young couple? See yourself walking up to the house where the wedding feast is to be held. Hear the sounds of the party. Feel the excitement you might experience at such an event.

As you walk into the courtyard, see yourself greeting old friends. Whom do you embrace? Can you hear the sounds of laughter? Do you sense the joy of the occasion?

Your good friend Mary moves toward you with delight on her face. "Come," she says, "I want you to meet my son, Jesus, and his friends." She takes your arm and leads you to a group of young men who are having an animated conversation.

"Jesus," Mary says to her son. A strong, handsome man turns gently to his mother. "I want you to meet my friend."

*Face to face with Jesus, at a party, what do you do?*

*What does he say to you?*

# Day 2

Return to the scene of the wedding in yesterday's meditation. Hear yourself carrying on a casual conversation with Jesus. See how he listens to you with rapt attention. Sense your feelings of warmth and safety as you banter with him about the wedding. Hear him introduce his friends to you.

Mary walks up to her son and tugs on his sleeve. Watch him bend down to hear her whispered words. She partially covers her mouth, but you can hear her.

"Jesus," she says, in her best Jewish mother's voice, "they have run out of wine. You know how embarrassing it is for the parents. Can you help them?"

Jesus looks at his mother with an expression you can't quite define. Is he surprised at her request? Is he irritated?

You look away, for you are embarrassed for Mary. What on earth does she have in mind? Whose responsibility is the wine, anyway?

"What do you mean?" Jesus asks her. "You know it isn't my time."

Mary calls for the servants to cooperate with Jesus. You can't help watching. What will happen next?

*Jesus looks at you and smiles.*

*You are puzzled, but intrigued.*

*What do you do?*

19

# Day 3

Imagine that you are one of the servants at the wedding party. You are embarrassed and humiliated for your master because he has run out of wine. Now, one of the guests has asked you to do whatever this man Jesus wants you to do.

You are weary, for you have been tending revelers for many hours. Feel the fatigue in your bones. How you would like just to clean up and go to your own quarters! Who is this woman telling you what to do?

Then Jesus comes to you, and when you look into his eyes, your resistance vanishes. There is something about him that makes you feel important. He is respectful to you, and as he tells you what to do, his words seem soothing.

He says, "Fill the waterpots with water."

It's a simple request, but it doesn't make much sense. He repeats the request, and you enlist the help of the other servants. There are six waterpots, and they are heavy.

Your friend says, "What is he going to do with all this water?"

You shrug. It doesn't seem to make much sense, but you fill the pots and move back into the presence of Jesus. Feel the ache in your back from the day's work.

*In your own life right now,*
*what is imperfect?*

*What is Jesus asking you to do*
*that doesn't make much sense?*

*Are you willing*
*to carry out the request of Jesus?*

# Day 4

Imagine that you, one of the servants in the household of the wedding feast, are standing before Jesus after filling the six waterpots with water. You are so tired, and you are puzzled. What is Jesus going to do now?

You hear the sounds of the party, and you know that most of the celebrants have no idea what is going on in this hallway. You sense that something important is about to happen. Jesus turns and looks deeply into your eyes. You can tell he is pleased that you have followed his unusual request.

Now, Jesus asks you to do something even more unusual. He asks you to draw out some of the water and take it to the headwaiter.

You can't believe it! You know how tired and grouchy the headwaiter gets after one of these wild Jewish wedding celebrations. And Jesus is asking you to take him a glass of water? He can't be serious!

Feel the discomfort of the moment. Do you try to talk Jesus out of this absurd idea? See the patience in his eyes as you waver between going and refusing. He understands your feelings and urges you to go ahead.

*Obedience on one point*
*opens up the next possibility.*

*Where in your life*
*do you need to obey the leading of Christ?*

*What will you do*
*about that need to obey?*

# *Day 5*

In your imagination, return to yesterday's scene. You are aware that the other servants are standing dumbstruck, waiting to see what you will do.

For some reason you cannot explain, you begin to dip the goblet down into the waterpot. Slowly, with your eyes on Jesus, you obey.

Feel the cool water on your hand. Jesus reaches out and touches your shoulder with approval and encouragement. You pause, wipe the goblet with a rough cloth, and look into his eyes. He tells you to go ahead and take it to the headwaiter.

Time stands still for a moment, but then you turn away and move slowly toward the headwaiter. In your mind, though, all you can see are those tender, smiling eyes of Jesus. You have no idea why this is the right thing to do, but you know, without a doubt, that it is.

The headwaiter takes the goblet from you, a frown of irritation wrinkling his face.

"Drink it," you tell him. And he does. You wait, afraid of his response.

"This wine," he says, "where did you get it? It's better than anything we have ever had here!"

*In what ways does Christ want to use you*
*to carry out his work today?*

*What does he want you to do for him?*

# Day 6

Today, see yourself again as the friend at the wedding party. You have just witnessed an amazing scene with Jesus and common water in common clay pots, and you don't know what to make of it.

Your mind is whirling. You know that you have seen something most unusual, and you are fascinated. Most of the people at the party take another glass of wine; they don't know where it came from.

Jesus comes and sits down beside you. You are filled with questions about what he does for a living and how he turned that water into wine, but you can't verbalize them. He seems to understand your feelings and respects your need to be still and ponder the events of the evening. Strangely, you feel quite comfortable in his presence.

"Give me your life," Jesus says suddenly. "Give me the parts that have become dull and boring and stale, and I will give you, in turn, the joy of life. I want to release you from anything that is holding you in bondage and give you peace, love, and joy."

"How will you do that?" you ask him, and then you remember the water that became wine. Before he responds, you know that he wants to bring richness and delight into your life.

"Give me your emptiness," he says, "and I will fill it."

*You look at Jesus closely.*

*He waits for your response.*

*What do you say?*

23

# Day 7

Imagine that you are Mary, the mother of Jesus. You have slipped outside for a breath of fresh air and a moment to think. You're trembling slightly as you ponder what your son has just done, and you smile. You hope you didn't press him too much; you knew what he could do, but you weren't sure he would do it. You hope he isn't upset with you.

As you stand in the evening breeze, you recall the night of his birth. Stretching further back in your memory, you recall that awesome moment when the angel startled you with his radical message. There you see Jesus throughout his growing-up years. You now recall the increasing power and presence he exhibits. Also, you see his gentleness and tenderness. He always has had an unusual understanding and grasp of human nature. How favored you are to call him your son!

Suddenly, your reverie is broken as Jesus touches you on the shoulder. You move closer to him, and he embraces you. You look into his eyes and know that you can ask him anything.

*What do you need to ask of Jesus right now?*

*Tell him,*
*and then wait in silence for his answer,*
*knowing that*
*he is all-sufficient and can meet every human need.*

# Feeding Crowds

Matthew 14:13-21
Mark 6:30-44
Luke 9:10-17
John 6:1-14

## Day 1

Take yourself back to a sunny day during the time of Jesus. Pretend that you live near the Sea of Galilee. See yourself walking beside the water, perhaps on a break from your work.

As you walk, you mull over a family crisis or a personal issue. You stretch your arms up in the air and breathe deeply of the sea breeze. The clear blue sky calms you. Reaching into your pocket, you pull out some dates for a snack.

You hear excited voices, and you turn to see what is causing the excitement. There is that man Jesus again. They say he performs miracles, and so you stop to watch. Your curiosity goads you into getting closer to him.

As you move toward Jesus, you think about all the things you need to finish today. You wonder if you should stay longer. After all, you really should get back to your responsibilities, but something draws you forward toward the Nazarene.

You notice that as Jesus sits down on the hillside, people rush to be close to him. You think it's interesting that he has time to stop, and that he lets people get so close to him.

*When Jesus starts to speak,*
*it is as if he is talking just to you.*

*What does he say?*

*Day 2*

Return in your imagination to the sunny hillside near the Sea of Galilee. You have been sitting on the green grass for quite some time; now you shift to a more comfortable position.

Also, you strain to hear every word Jesus says. You are intrigued by the probing questions of the crowd; now and then, you are even shocked by some of the things people ask! You have wondered about a lot of life's mysteries, but you had never dared to ask about them.

Notice how patient Jesus is with the crowd. You sense that he is fully present to each one and that he understands their deepest longings. He treats each person with respect and love.

You become aware that part of the reason Jesus draws such a crowd is that he understands the complexities of life. He knows about the conflicts that rise up between people. He sees beyond the superficial problems or symptoms to the real issues of fear, guilt, inferiority, hate, and anger. He wants to give answers that will solve the problems and not merely relieve the symptoms.

*As you sit on the hillside,
what questions do you want to ask Jesus?*

*Can you sense his love and care for you?*

*Do you know that you are his Father's child
and that he takes great delight in who you are?*

*Do you know that he is glad to be with you?*

# *Day 8*

As you sit on the hillside with the crowd, you become aware that the day is slipping away. You are startled to realize that you have been so long in one place and have shirked your responsibilities. You stir, look around you, and see that the entire crowd is still there.

A child in front of you cries, "I'm hungry, Mama," and you smile. You are hungry too, and yet you realize that sitting in the presence of Jesus has satisfied a hunger far deeper than the physical.

Jesus hears the child and smiles and calls the child to him. You watch Jesus bend over and lift the child into his arms. The child tells Jesus he is hungry, and Jesus assures him that he will take care of his need.

You watch Jesus turn to his friend Philip and ask him about feeding the hungry crowd. You see Philip shrug, and you think you sense impatience among the rest of Jesus' friends. After all, they must have wanted Jesus just for themselves.

When you hear Philip's reply, you realize there isn't any point in staying, and so you stand up, brush the grass off your clothes, and start to leave.

*What is your deepest hunger at this time in your life?*

*What need do you want Christ to fill today?*

*What need does Jesus want to meet in you?*

*When confronted with a problem,
do you focus on your limitations
or on Christ's limitless power?*

# Day 4

As you stand there, poised between leaving and staying, your curiosity is piqued by Andrew, one of Jesus' friends. For you hear Andrew telling Jesus that a boy has five barley loaves and two fish, and frankly, you are a little embarrassed for Andrew. Does he plan to feed himself and leave everyone else hungry? Besides, who would want the common food of barley loaves and those fish? And how could Andrew think of taking a small boy's meal from him?

You turn again to leave, but then you notice Jesus is calling his friends to come to him. You wonder if they are arguing, for they are quite animated. One of them walks away, shaking his head, but then he turns and goes back to the circle.

You see the little boy walk right up to Jesus and hold out his lunch, and you want to cry. How generous of the child to offer the great teacher some lunch!

*Think about your own life right now.*
*What very common thing might Jesus want to use*
*to bring about good for you?*

*Could there be something right in front of you*
*that you have overlooked that he wants to use to feed you?*

*Is there some person you hadn't counted on*
*who might be a source of nurture?*

*Is there one argument you keep having with Jesus?*

*Do you spend enough time with Christ for him to feed you,*
*or do you rush on to your responsibilities?*

# *Day 5*

There you are on the hillside with thousands of hungry people. You need to get back to work, but you don't want to
leave. You sense something unusual is about to happen, and
you don't want to miss it. Besides, the crowd is so thick, you
can't get through the people to go home.

You inch a little closer to Jesus and can't believe your
ears when he tells his friends to have the people sit down.
How does he think anyone could calm this noisy crowd?

The disciples question Jesus further, but then they turn
and move through the crowd, asking the people to sit down.
You watch in amazement as the crowd does what they ask.
Even you find a place to sit!

The crowd waits in silence. All eyes are fixed on Jesus
as he bends down and whispers something in the ear of the
small boy who offered his lunch. The boy smiles and stands
up so straight and proud. He runs back to his mother and
sits down beside her. The mother asks him questions, but
the boy says, "Shhh, you'll see."

*Are you in the midst of a perplexing time?*

*Is God's timetable strange and slow to you?*

*Are you impatiently waiting for God to do something,
and you don't understand the delay?*

*Can you wait for the Living Christ,
secure in the knowledge that his will for you is perfect?*

*Can you let go of your preconceived expectations
and let him do as he wills?*

# Day 6

Watch closely now! Jesus is taking the five loaves in his strong hands. Watch him hold them up toward the heavens and hear him give thanks for them.

What will he do next? The crowd waits, as if on tiptoe with expectation. Jesus lifts the two fish and gives thanks for them as if they were the banquet of a rich man.

Then he and his friends begin moving through the crowd, distributing food, and you are thunderstruck with awe!

When he comes to you, you hold out your hands, and he fills them with more than enough for you. He looks into your eyes, and his presence itself feels like all-sufficiency. You think that you will never know another need, now that you have been filled with the love of Jesus.

As he moves on, you place the tender morsels in your mouth. You eat all you want and are completely satisfied. You glance around you and notice that everyone is filled. The crowd is marveling and exclaiming about the food. How did it happen? Where did that abundance come from?

*What is Christ longing to offer you today?*

*What abundance has he been trying to give you?*

*Will you accept his gift of Living Bread,*
*the constant assurance of his presence with you?*

# Day 7

You know you have lingered on the hillside long enough. You must return to the responsibilities of family and work, and so you get up and begin walking through the milling crowd.

Now and then, you stop and share with a friend the marvel of the meal you have just had. You embrace each other, caught up in the warmth of the miracle you have experienced together. You notice how much easier it is to extend love when you have been loved and nurtured.

You realize with surprise that Jesus' friends are picking up the abundance of the leftovers. Where there was nothing only moments before, now there is excess.

Moving back into your own daily routine, you ponder the entire experience. You feel as if the scales have been removed from your eyes and you see things you have never seen before. Your mind whirls and tumbles with new insights. You understand now that if you will bring your resources to him, he can multiply whatever you have and use it to help others.

*What difference will this experience make in the way you live?*

*Who are the human instruments Jesus has used to feed you? Take a moment and give thanks for them.*

*Whom does Jesus want to bless through you?*

*Are you willing to be his instrument of blessing, healing, and loving?*

*Thank him for all he has done for you.*

*Fear Not . . .*
*It Is I!*

Mark 6:47-52

# Day 1

See yourself walking with Jesus' friends beside a lake. You are part of his group of special friends. On this day, he has fed thousands of people with the lunch of a little boy, and now all of you are hoping to spend some time with Jesus away from the crowds.

Picture the late evening sun on the lake. Listen to the lap of the water on the shore. See your friends pulling a boat up to land and climbing in. Feel the water on your feet and the breeze on your face.

"Where did Jesus go?" one of the friends asks. Another replies, "He went back up into the mountain to pray."

"He's always going off by himself," one complains.

"He says he must spend time with his Father," you tell them, but all the time you wonder why he has to go so often.

You climb into the boat and find a place to sit. You lean back against the side and close your eyes. So much has happened today, and there is so much to process. You want to talk about it with the others, but everyone seems strangely reticent.

Wearily, you close your eyes and rub your forehead. You wait for Jesus to return. Suddenly, it becomes clear to you that there is a connection between Jesus' power and the time he spends off by himself.

*If Jesus had to seek solitude*
*to stay connected to the Source,*
*what about you?*

# *Day 2*

Return to the scene in the boat. As you and the others who have been with Jesus set out across the lake for Capernaum, night falls.

Nobody speaks, but you know that everyone is wishing Jesus were with you in the boat. Imagine what it is like to be out in a boat in the dark.

The wind begins to blow, and you inhale deeply the scent of coming rain. Suddenly, all your senses are heightened—you have been out on this lake often enough to know when there is danger.

Now the wind gathers force, and the ones who are rowing strain at the oars, shouting to each other over the roar of the storm. You reach out to help. The power of the wind against the small boat calls for all the strength you have.

"Where is Jesus now?" one of the rowers demands in a harsh, frightened voice. "You'd think he would care as much about us as he did all of those strangers he fed this afternoon!"

*In reality,*
*there may be high winds beating on the boat of your life.*
*It may seem that you are being tossed about*
*by the currents of change.*
*Disasters or worries may be about to capsize you,*
*and you may wonder where Jesus is,*
*now that you really need him.*

*What waves are beating on your boat?*

*Do you really believe*
*that Jesus knows where you are in your storm?*

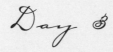

# Day 3

Return in your imagination to the storm on the lake. Recall your feelings about being tossed about by the storm and abandoned by Jesus.

Suddenly Jesus appears, seemingly out of nowhere, walking on the water toward your boat. Stunned, you cry out to the others to look into the storm. Can it really be Jesus? Maybe it's just your imagination. Can it be that he has come to help?

The others are alarmed. They aren't sure this is Jesus. It could be a ghost! They scream in terror. You, however, know that this is Jesus coming to you in the midst of your storm.

Even while Jesus was praying on the mountain, he was not really away from the disciples. He always knew what was going on with them at each moment. He knew their need and was able to meet that need at the right time.

Jesus knew the big picture. He saw the toil of the disciples as they were trying to save themselves. He saw their fatigue and terror, and he knew the extent of the danger.

*In your life,*
*Jesus knows every detail of your own personal storm.*

*He knows every need you have.*

*He senses your feelings.*

*He knows what you are doing to try to save yourself.*

*All the time, he is interceding on your behalf to the Father.*

*What is Jesus' prayer for you right now?*

# Day 4

In your imagination, think what it would be like to be out on a dark lake in a terrible storm. What thoughts would rush through your mind? How would your body feel as you wrestle with the boat, trying to keep it from filling with water? Let yourself feel alone and afraid.

Now you see Jesus walking toward you in the storm. What does it do to your spirit to recognize him coming toward you on the water? What do you do when you see him? What do you say?

Jesus took the initiative to move toward the disciples in their time of need, and he takes the initiative to come to his friends now through the power of the Holy Spirit. He is never absent, nor does he ever lose sight of any of his children.

Imagine that you are sitting with Jesus right now, telling him about the struggles of your life. He listens to every word you say and takes your feelings seriously. He is never too busy to hear you, and he doesn't interrupt when you are speaking.

*How does it feel to have the full attention of Jesus?*

*How does it feel to tell him the story of your life without any censure or ridicule?*

*How does it feel to have the Son of God with you and on your side?*

*As you sit with Jesus, allow him to speak to you about your challenges or troubles.*

*Listen to him as respectfully as he listens to you.*

# *Day 5*

Move your attention back to the moment when you saw the figure of Jesus walking toward your boat. Imagine this time that you are one of the disciples who doesn't recognize him but thinks he is a ghost.

For a moment, feel the fear that blinds you to Jesus' true identity. Experience the confusion that keeps you from seeing things clearly. Another disciple tries to calm you by telling you that Jesus is coming to you, but you refuse to believe him. He tries to convince you that it is the Master, but you won't let go of your fear long enough to recognize him.

There are times when fear paralyzes our minds and feelings, forcing us to stay locked in our troubles. Fear keeps us from seeing the hand of God when it is right before us, stilling the storm and calming our hearts.

Imagine that you gather up just enough courage to be still and to look for the presence of Christ. When you are in the middle of a storm, take several deep breaths. Close your eyes and remember his words to the disciples, "Fear not! . . . It is I."

*Jesus will identify himself to you*
*in the midst of your storms.*

*What keeps you from hearing and recognizing*
*the sound of his voice?*
*What makes you hold on to your fear?*

*Isn't the power of Christ greater than any other power?*
*Isn't Christ's love greater than all your fear?*

*Let him love you.*

# Day 6

In your imagination, watch Jesus climb into the boat and sit down among you and your friends. What do you feel when he does this?

As he sits down, the wind begins to subside. The waters gradually become calm. The clouds part and seem to dissipate before your eyes, revealing a full moon in a clear sky.

Your friends who have been straining and pulling at the oars, trying to keep the boat stable, fall exhausted to the deck. You look around, counting heads to make sure everyone is there.

Jesus looks at each of you and calls you by name as if he, too, wants to make sure that each one is in place. You hear him call your name, and you look up into his face. He gazes at you with such compassion and concern.

Jesus has walked into the chaos and created peace. He has done for you what you could not do for yourself. He has saved you from disaster. Relief wells up in your throat, and you weep for joy.

*What would it look like if Jesus walked into*
*your present circumstances and created peace?*

*Where would the peace be made?*
*What waves would he calm?*

*How would you feel, looking up into his face*
*as he stilled your personal storm?*

*Jesus wants to bring peace into your life,*
*regardless of your circumstances.*
*Imagine that he is doing that even now.*

# Day 7

Return in your imagination to the moment when Jesus stilled the storm and the boat was saved from overturning. See your friends pick up their oars and begin to row silently toward the shore.

Feel yourself reach for your own oar and pick it up. You thought you wouldn't have strength left to row to shore, but you are filled with new energy and a strange kind of power. The day's events flash through your mind as you hear the rhythmic slap of the oars on the water.

You turn and look at Jesus. Who is this man, anyway? You have seen him turn water into wine and feed thousands with a small lunch. Now he has mysteriously appeared in the middle of the storm to save your life.

Even stranger is the incredible peace you sense. Not only has the storm been calmed, but you feel peaceful inside. It is a feeling you have been searching for all your life. Now you realize that the deep confidence and trust you have in Jesus has brought you great peace.

You watch Jesus as he rests in the boat. In his presence, even while he is asleep, your heart is at rest. You know what serenity is, and with that serenity is a deep wellspring of joy. In Jesus' presence, there is no fear.

*How can you remain in the presence of Christ?*

*He is always there, actually.*

*Do you know that?*

# First Love

JOHN 4:1-32

*Day 1*

As you enter into today's meditation, imagine that you are one of Jesus' disciples. You are traveling with him through Samaria, and you stop in a village called Sychar.

Imagine the heat of the noonday sun beating down on your head. Look down at your feet and see the dust on your sandals. Feel the dryness of your mouth, the stinging in your eyes, the ache of fatigue in your body.

You and the others did not want to travel through Samaria. Jesus hasn't tried to argue you out of your prejudices but has simply ignored your resistance and your protests. Now he, a Jewish man, walks straight into the middle of the village to the well.

See yourself standing over to the side, in the shade of a building. For a moment, you lean against the building and close your eyes. When you hear Jesus talking, you open your eyes and are stunned that he is speaking not only to a Samaritan, but to a woman! As you watch the exchange and hear what is said, you realize that this woman has a bad reputation.

All the things you have been taught about propriety and good judgment tumble around in your head. Does Jesus know what he is doing? Doesn't he realize that he'll get himself in trouble?

*In what areas of your life*
*is Christ trying to move you beyond your prejudices?*

*Who is the Samaritan woman for you?*

# *Day 2*

Using the God-given gift of seeing with the mind's eye, return to the scene from yesterday. This time, however, imagine that you are the Samaritan woman approaching Jacob's well.

You have come at high noon because that is the time of day when the other women are at home, and you can avoid their stares and cutting comments. You cover as much of your face as you can to give yourself some privacy. Your mind is filled with your problems; your heart is heavy with the burdens of life.

Feel the rough texture of the heavy water pot you carry to the well. Using your sleeve, you wipe the perspiration from your forehead. You hurry—you don't want to be caught at the well by the other women.

Imagine your distress when you see a Jewish man sitting by the well. You look down and mutter your frustration to yourself, pulling your covering closer around your face.

As you begin to dip into the well for the cool water, the man speaks to you. At first, you don't believe your ears, but he speaks again. Your heart clenches; he must know about your reputation. You decide to ignore him.

Again, he speaks, asking for a drink of water.

*Jesus comes to each person,*
*regardless of reputation or history.*

*What do you want to hide from the Savior?*

43

# Day 8

Identify again with the disciple who is watching the scene at the well. As you stand amazed, Jesus carries on quite a conversation with this woman of questionable character.

You call to one of the other disciples. He has fallen asleep, leaning against a tree. You startle him, but when he realizes what Jesus is doing, he becomes fully awake.

You and the disciple debate with each other. Should you go and rescue Jesus from this woman? Should you divert his attention? What will people think if it gets around that Jesus talks openly with women such as this?

As you watch the conversation, however, you sense that something important is going on. Jesus shows great respect to the woman, and she gradually responds to that respect with dignity and openness. What is it about Jesus that makes people open up to him?

Jesus gives good news to all who have ears to hear, crossing all the boundaries that human beings erect. He breaks whatever rules he needs to break to give salvation to the lost.

*In the silence, allow the Living Christ*
*to tell you where the Spirit is working in your culture.*

*Are you encouraging the freedom of his activity?*

*Are you helping him, or are you hindering his work?*

*Ask Christ to show you how*
*to take the good news beyond your comfort zone.*

*Day 4*

Identify again with the woman at the well. Hear Jesus request a drink of water. Because of your many relationships with men, your first thoughts jump to what he may really want from you. You stick out your chin in defiance and look straight up into his eyes.

You are expecting a sneer, perhaps, or a look of contempt. You think he may be looking at you in that arrogant, demanding way the other men in your life look at you. But the look in Jesus' eyes startles you. It is like no other you have ever seen from a man. For the first time in your life you see utter love and acceptance in the eyes of another human being, and you cannot take your eyes away. You feel safe and valuable. Simply standing there in his presence, you are different.

*In the silence today,*
*imagine that Jesus looks at you with the eyes of love.*

*He has come to you to change your life, to make it better,*
*to take all your brokenness and turn it into beauty.*

*What is your response,*
*as you let Jesus look into your eyes?*

*Do you want to turn away,*
*or are you comfortable with his nearness to you?*

*What do you say to Jesus when he draws near?*

*What does he say to you?*

45

# Day 5

Imagine again that you are the Samaritan woman at the well in Sychar. Feel yourself leaning against the rough side of the well. See yourself holding your water pot against your body. Hear your voice as you remind this Jewish man that you and he shouldn't even be talking to each other.

You turn to complete your task of filling your water pot, assuming the man will stop talking. You decide to ignore him, but he says something about "living water," as if he has access to some special water. Doesn't he realize that this well provided pure water centuries before he ever came on the scene? You tell him about your forefather, Jacob, who gave the well to your ancestor, hoping to put him in his place.

The man keeps on talking and goes so far as to say that he can give you water that will quench your thirst forever! What a claim! You laugh at him. But he won't quit talking about this "living water!"

"So, give me some of this water," you challenge him, and you look at him with insolence. Can he back up his offer?

*Ask the Spirit of Christ to reveal to you*
*the ways you try to argue God out of his gift for you.*

*How do your skepticism and cynicism*
*get in the way of Christ's gift of grace to you?*

*How do guilt and shame about your past*
*keep you from accepting the forgiveness he wants to give?*

# Day 6

Return to the scene at the well. You, as the Samaritan wo-man, start to leave the well. The Jewish man hasn't come forth with this living water, and you want to go home.

"Bring your husband," he says to you, and your heart stops. You don't look at him but toss your reply over your shoulder. "I don't have a husband."

You start to move away, but stop when he begins telling you about your life. He knows about your past. He knows all the details, and yet, he's not condemning you, and he isn't trying to get something from you. This man is speaking in love and is offering to give you something!

You decide he must be a prophet. You try to change the subject by talking about the different places of worship. As he continues talking to you, patiently answering you, you become aware of his power and authority.

You decide to walk away, but before you go, you tell him you know that the Messiah will explain everything when he comes. The man says, "I am he." You look into his eyes, and it's as if the whole world stands still. Colors are brighter, and sounds are sharper. Your heart is set free from the shackles of the past! He knows you, yet he loves you!

*In your mind's eye,*
*see Jesus look past all your defenses and pretenses*
*to the real you.*

*Hear him say,*
*"I love you."*

# Day 7

You, the Samaritan woman, put your water pot down on the ground and run toward your home. Thoughts and memories race through your mind as you run.

This man's "water" is the answer to all your searching. This man and his love are so much greater than all the imperfect, hurting loves you have had with your many husbands. Today, at the well, you have found what you have been searching for in one man after another.

You think back to when you began selling out to others. You recall the times you let men become god to you, doing what they wanted even though it didn't ever feel right. You weep as you remember how desperately you searched for security and meaning and belonging. This love you have found today is the only love that matters! The past isn't erased, exactly, but it is as if all the wounds of your heart have been cleansed and healed.

You go from house to house, calling to your neighbors to come to the well and meet the man who knows you, yet loves you! You take the covering away from your face and look straight into the eyes of your neighbors. No longer do you hide. No longer must you live in shame. Now you have good news to tell!

*What are you hiding from Christ?*

*Tell him that you know he knows all about you.*

*Accept his unconditional love.*

*Find someone who needs to make a trip to the well.*

# Rise . . .
## and Walk

MATTHEW 9:1-8
MARK 2:1-12
LUKE 5:17-26

*Day 1*

Today, imagine you are a Pharisee or teacher of the law in Jesus' day. Get in touch with that feeling of being right.

You are sitting in the home of a friend with other Pharisees and teachers where you have been invited to listen to this teacher, Jesus. Because it is your job to protect the traditions and teachings, you have come. You need to know why Jesus is attracting such a following. You have to admit that he is engaging. It's just hard to believe that love is so crucial.

You resist Jesus' words. You argue with him, and you side with the others who debate his teachings. Finally, you sit back in your chair and look around the room at the others to measure their responses to this radical man.

You notice that one of your friends is smiling and agreeing with Jesus. Has he been won over? How do you feel about this?

Another friend sits outside the circle and is sullen and restless. You know he wants to leave. What would you say to him?

*Jesus turns to you and looks straight into your eyes.*

*"What do you think about these things?" he asks you.*

# *Day 2*

As you read again the Scripture for the week, imagine that you are a friend of a paralytic. You have seen your friend suffer for years, and you've tried to help him.

Imagine that another friend comes rushing into your home one day and asks you to go with him to take your paralyzed friend to the man Jesus whom you have heard can heal the sick.

Do you respond eagerly to your friend's suggestions? Or do you try to talk him out of it? Is your first response one of caution or of eager hope? You decide to go with your friend. After all, it won't hurt to try, will it?

You move through the streets to your friend's house, picking up two other friends to help you carry him on his mat. How do you feel as you go into the lame man's home and tell him that you are going to take him to Jesus? What do you say to convince your friend that this is a good thing for you to do? What are the thoughts that move through your mind as you walk through the streets toward the house where Jesus is teaching? Do you worry about what other people will think? What if it doesn't work? What if it does?

*Who in your life needs to be*
*taken in prayer to Jesus for healing?*

*What friend of yours might be depending on you to tell him*
*about the only source of real and permanent healing?*

*Day 3*

Put yourself on the mat of the paralytic. Try to feel what it is like to spend your lifetime paralyzed and unable to care for yourself. Imagine what it is like to be completely dependent on another person.

You have spent this day like hundreds of others. Then suddenly, some friends burst through the door. They are excited and animated, talking quickly and moving fast toward you.

"We are going to take you to Jesus," they tell you. "We think he can heal you." And they begin picking up the four corners of your mat.

How do you respond? Do you argue with them, telling them about all the ways you've tried to be healed throughout your life? Do you beg them to be easy with you, for every move is painful? Do you eagerly accept their effort, hopeful that this might be the answer to your lifelong problem?

As your friends move through the streets with you in tow, your mind is whirling with possibilities. The houses of your street go by in a flash. You beg your friends to slow down. You hope they won't drop you!

*Is there some part of your life that is lame?*

*Are you paralyzed with*
*fear, guilt, anger, hate, or feelings of inadequacy?*

# Day 4

Imagine that you are the owner of the house in which Jesus is teaching. You've gone out on a limb to invite your friends. Many of them aren't sure what to think of this new teacher.

You listen to Jesus teaching about being a part of the kingdom of God. You sit apart from your guests, watching them debate and question Jesus. You're fascinated with the way he handles the arguments. He allows them to say what they want to and doesn't condemn them for holding other opinions. He just keeps coming back to love and forgiveness and service.

You hear an uproar outside, but there are so many people crowded in the room and at each door and window that you don't attempt to see what is happening. All of a sudden, the thatched roof right above Jesus is lifted.

Appalled, you rise to your feet; but before you can protest, a man on a mat is lowered down right in front of Jesus! The crowd is aghast; you can hear a pin drop. It is so quiet!

You look at Jesus. Surely, as the host, you should make some kind of explanation or apology; but when you see his face, you realize that he is perfectly in control, even of this surprise encounter. He is looking with absolute compassion and tenderness at the paralyzed man huddled at his feet.

*Is some human need disrupting your life right now?*

*What would Jesus say to you about that need?*

## Day 5

Today, become the lame man again, as you lie at the feet of Jesus. Your heart is beating wildly, as much from fear and embarrassment as from the rushed trip on your mat and the scary descent through the roof!

Be aware of how it feels to be the center of attention, an uninvited guest plunged down into the middle of a crowded room. You who have spent your life avoiding the scrutiny of others now are in full view. You who have become accustomed to the privacy of your mat of affliction now are exposed to the very ones who have said that your problem is the result of sin.

Jesus must sense your embarrassment, for he glances quickly up at your friends who are peering down at you through the hole in the roof and then leans down and touches you. "Friend," he calls you, and you look at him with astonishment. This great teacher calls you "friend"!

"Your sins are forgiven," Jesus tells you, and you hear a stir of discord in the room. You know the people can't believe their ears.

"Rise up," Jesus tells you. "Take your mat and go home."

You don't hesitate, but you're filled with amazement. You slowly stand up in front of the whole crowd! Feel every move. Suddenly, you can walk!

*Is a part of your emotional, physical, relational, intellectual, or spiritual life paralyzed and in need of a healing word from Jesus?*

# Day 6

You are a Pharisee who is witnessing the healing of the paralytic. Imagine your astonishment as the lame man is lowered to the floor. See the people around Jesus scatter to make room for this surprise intruder. What are your reactions as Jesus leans down and touches this man whom you have avoided?

You are shocked to hear Jesus turn the sacred beliefs of your forefathers upside down in a flash when he tells the man his sins are forgiven. Then you hear him tell the paralytic to get up and walk. Who is this Jesus who says and does things that challenge every tradition you have spent your life upholding and defending? Who does he think he is to come into your village and claim to do what God alone can do?

Watch in disbelief as the lame man rises to his feet. See the stunned looks on the faces of the man's neighbors and friends. Most important, watch Jesus' face. You have never before seen that expression on the face of any rabbi or teacher. It seems to be a look of pure love.

What will you do with this man Jesus? Now that you have seen him heal someone, what will you do with your legalism? And how in the world will you relate to the lame man who can now walk?

*In the quietness,*
*ask the Holy Spirit of Christ to reveal to you*
*any blindness you may have to Jesus' signs and wonders.*

*Day 7*

In your imagination, identify with the paralytic as he stands in the middle of the crowd. You are looking down at your feet. You take one cautious step forward and then another and another.

The crowd parts in front of you to give you room. They smile at you, and you smile back at them. You head straight for the door and the open air. What will it be like to walk on the earth for the first time in your life?

You are keenly aware of the voices around you. You hear a sob in the corner, and you know it is a friend weeping for joy. You hear others praising God. Various ones call out encouragement, and you keep on walking.

As you move out into the sunlight, pause a moment and feel the exhilaration of being healed. Look out into the village where you have been carried from place to place. What freedom you feel. Now you can walk wherever you choose.

You step into the open air. Stand up tall and stretch toward the sun. How does it feel to be free?

*Ask Christ to give you the courage*
*to make the changes you need to make in your daily life.*

*Ask him to take responsibility*
*for the grace he has worked in your life.*

*Imagine what your life will be like*
*without the paralysis of sin.*

# Just Once More

LUKE 5:1-11

# *Day 1*

Think about a time when you expended a great deal of energy, time, and perhaps money on a particular project, only to have it fail. Recall a time when you felt you were spinning your wheels in your marriage or your work.

Imagine now that you are Simon Peter, the big fisherman, cleaning your nets at the edge of the Sea of Gennesaret. Feel the water lapping around your feet and legs. You're very tired after having fished all night; you're discouraged after having caught nothing.

While you clean your nets, Jesus sits in your boat, teaching the people who are on the shore. You do not listen to what he's saying until you hear him call your name. Then you look up, shading your weary eyes against the morning sunlight. Jesus tells you to go back out into the deep water and put your nets down again.

Disbelieving, you mutter, "What could a carpenter know about fishing? He hasn't been out there all night like we have! Who is he to tell us to get back out in the boats?"

*In the quietness,*
*ask the Living Christ to move through*
*your fatigue and discouragement*
*and tell you what to do next.*

*Ask him to give you*
*the energy to do what needs to be done.*

# *Day 2*

Return to the scene of yesterday's meditation. Jesus is teaching the people from your boat while you, Simon Peter, are standing at the shoreline, nets in hand.

You protest the carpenter's suggestion that you return to the lake. You tell him all the reasons it will not work. See the expression on his face as he listens to you. He understands why you hesitate, but he wants you to obey.

You walk closer to Jesus. You tell him how tired you are, how you worked all last night, and how discouraged you are because none of your best efforts produced any results. You want to walk away from Jesus, but something stops you. You can't explain it, but you decide to try one more time. The hard part, though, will be convincing the others.

You walk over to the others and tell them that you are going back out on the lake. What do they do? What do they say?

*What does Jesus want you to do now*
*that you don't want to do?*

*Where do you need to try*
*just one more time for him?*

*What part of your life*
*needs one more effort?*

*Day 3*

Once again you are Simon at the lake. You're working with the others to get the boats back onto the lake. There is silence as you work. You're all tired and wondering why you're going back out. As you push the boat out onto the lake, you feel the cold water on your legs.

You climb in and begin to row. Every stroke is an effort. Your weary muscles are heavy and sluggish. You try to encourage the others. "What do we have to lose?" you ask. What is their response to you?

You realize how unlikely it is that you'll catch any fish, and yet for some reason, you have hope. One of the other fishermen tells you again that the facts are against you. How do you respond to him? How do you explain this effort that seems contrary to reality? Do you think about what you will tell the others if you still don't succeed? What will they say? Do you care? Do you have the strength to try again?

You're not sure why you feel compelled to obey Jesus, but you do. It's the most important thing right now.

*In what area of your life does Jesus want you*
*to cast your net a little deeper?*

*Day 4*

Return again to the boat where you, Simon Peter the fisherman, are carrying out the instructions of Jesus, the carpenter.

As you move out in your boat into the water, you feel the morning sun beating down on your body. Breathe deeply and inhale the familiar smells of the sea. Feel the roughness of the boat against your feet, your arms, your body. Imagine the rocking of the boat in the water.

Now you lower the net into the water. Everyone begins to struggle with their nets. From out of nowhere the fish have come, filling your nets to overflowing. You begin bringing in the fish, and there are so many that the load nearly capsizes the boat. Where were all these fish last night?

The other fishermen are shouting to each other. You hear their laughter and shouts of amazement and delight. You laugh, too. How much easier it is to go home with a catch!

Now, look toward the shore and meet the eyes of Jesus. You want to ask him where the fish came from when they weren't there last night. But then your curiosity is lost in the realization that Jesus knew what you should do to bring in an abundant catch. It was his direction and your obedience that brought success.

*Ask Jesus for the courage to obey his guidance.*

# Day 5

Once the boat is full, you, Simon, and the other fishermen struggle to row the boat into shore. As soon as you are close enough, you jump out, leaving the others to bring in the fish. You no longer feel the fatigue of the night, and you know that they don't either. What you don't know is whether or not the others recognize that a miracle has taken place because you have obeyed Jesus.

You rush to the place where Jesus is standing, fall down on your knees in the sand, and tell him that you don't deserve his blessings because of your lack of obedience and trust. You thank him for blessing you, in spite of your disbelief.

Feel Jesus' hand in yours as he pulls you to your feet. He puts his hands on your shoulders and looks into your eyes.

"Don't be afraid," he tells you, and for the first time you realize that your lack of trust and your resistance to obeying him is, after all, a sign of fear.

As you stand before the carpenter who knows about fishing, recall the things you fear. Take an account of what you tell yourself that keeps you from obeying Christ. Think about the times he has blessed you in spite of your disobedience. See the mercy in his eyes.

*Ask Christ to remove all your resistance*
*to following him.*

*Ask him to make you ready*
*to be blessed by him.*

# Day 6

It's early morning. As you walk down to the shore of the sea, a crisp breeze blows against your face. You move toward your boat and become aware of the carpenter from Nazareth and his friends nearby. You have heard about them, but you don't know them. The carpenter is urging his friends to return to the sea for another try at catching fish. You become so intrigued by what they are saying that you are distracted from your work.

You watch as the disciples struggle with whether or not they are going to follow Jesus' suggestions. Then they get into their boats. You hear yourself joking with your friends about how foolish Jesus' disciples are to go back out. You turn back to your own work, making fun of Jesus and his friends. People need to know when it's time to give up; if the fish aren't biting, they aren't biting!

Working with your nets, you hear shouts and laughter, and turning toward the lake, you are shocked by the catch in the boats of the foolish men who wouldn't give up. You rush over to them; their excitement is contagious.

How could the man Jesus know where the fish were? What is it about him that would make professional fishermen listen to him and return to the lake after a long night of no fish?

*Do you envy someone*
*because of their relationship with Jesus?*

*Does Jesus want the same with you?*

# Day 7

In your imagination, see yourself again as Simon Peter. As you pull your boat up onto the shore, you have the sense that nothing in your life is ever going to be the same again.

As you work with the abundance of fish, you pay only partial attention to the bantering of the other fishermen. You are absorbed in your thoughts about the miracle you have just witnessed and about Jesus who made it happen.

You keep hearing Jesus' words, and you mull them over and over. What did he mean when he said that from now on you would "catch men"?

You know that now you have to make a choice. You have seen something you have never seen before. You have met a man unlike any other you have ever known. You have felt a power and a love like nothing you dreamed possible. You know already that you are changed. How will you explain this to your family and friends? Being the practical sort, you know that it won't do any good to tell people; the best thing to do is to live the changes.

You look up at Jesus and realize that he is waiting for you. Are you going to follow him? You make your choice; you stand up and go with Jesus.

*Ask Christ to give you the grace to follow him.*

# A Hungering Listener

LUKE 10:38-42

# *Day 1*

During the years of his ministry, Jesus stressed hospitality. Perhaps he did this because he knew that this practice would be crucial in the establishment of the early church. Much of the sharing of new life would take place as fellow Christians welcomed each other into their homes.

Jesus knew personally the joy of visiting in a friend's home. Yet, because of the nature of his ministry, there were places he was not welcome; therefore, those who received him into their homes were especially important to him.

At the home of his friends Mary and Martha and their brother Lazarus, Jesus spent happy hours.

Imagine that you are there when Jesus visits the home of these friends. See him interacting with them. Can you hear the gentle teasing that often accompanies relaxed, casual gatherings of friends who love and trust each other? Can you see the concern in their faces as he relates the various challenges of his ministry? Do you hear him inquiring about their problems?

*Is Jesus welcome in your home?*

*Do you want to hide any part of your life from him?*

*What family concerns do you want to tell him about?*

# Day 2

There are many ways Luke could have described Mary, the sister of Martha and Lazarus. What he chose to tell us was that she was "listening to the Lord."

Imagine that you are in that small home in Bethany, sitting at the feet of Jesus. Imagine that you are Mary. You know that women of your day are expected to be busy with preparing the meals, but you choose to go against the norm and sit in a room with the men, listening to what a Jewish teacher has to say.

As Mary, do you sit right in front of him, or are you more reserved, moving a little distance away? Are you quiet, or do you dare ask questions and interject your opinions and thoughts?

Imagine Jesus' response to you as you ask him a question. See him give you, a woman, unconditional positive regard and respect. He looks directly into your eyes. He listens carefully and gives you time to say everything you want to say. He doesn't laugh at you or discount your questions. Jesus takes you seriously! How does this feel?

You hear in his voice Jesus' concern for you. He is joyful when you understand what he is saying about abundant life. As you or Lazarus speaks, Jesus looks into your face, giving you his undivided attention. Jesus wants to understand, and he wants to be understood.

*How does it feel to dialogue with Jesus?*

## *Day 3*

The household of Mary and Martha is busy as the evening meal is being prepared. Martha's helpers are setting the table. The simmering stew and baking bread smell good.

Again, you are Mary, sitting at the feet of Jesus, oblivious to all else going on in the house. You are absorbed in what he says. Your desire for his message has been like an intense hunger or thirst, and his words satisfy the deepest longing of your heart.

Suddenly, the words of your sister, Martha, pierce the air, and a familiar guilt washes over you. Immediately, you berate yourself for neglecting your duties. You are embarrassed because your shortcomings are now out in the open for everyone, especially Jesus, to see. You swallow your anger toward your sister, but you know that you will pay for spending time with Jesus.

What do you do? Do you apologize for not helping Martha in the kitchen? Do you rush about, making up for your neglect? Do you pout, wallowing in self-pity for not being understood and feeling embarrassed at being publicly censured? Or do you feel that there is no need for an explanation and so quietly assume your duty?

*While Jesus never calls you to irresponsibility,*
*following him calls for a radical change in your priorities.*

*What challenge will you face if you spend time with Jesus?*

*Day 4*

Jesus could always see through the apparent problem and move deeper into the real issue. Jesus healed at the deepest level by always addressing the causes of problems and not just the symptoms.

Again as Mary, you are stopped in your tracks as Jesus addresses your sister, Martha. Can it be that he is saying to her the very things you have tried to say? You look at your sister whom you love and know so well. Your love is mixed with a lifetime of family "stuff." Can it be that Jesus is taking care of a problem that has been an ongoing barrier between the two of you? As he talks, the tension between the two of you is released. You no longer harbor resentment for how she doesn't understand you. Let your compassion for Martha fill your heart. You feel her pain and sense the hunger and thirst in her heart.

*The presence of the Living Christ can take care of*
*the most difficult or trifling relationship problems.*

*Because he cares about all our lives,*
*he wants to restore relationships,*
*beginning with those closest to us.*

*What close relationship*
*does Christ want to heal for you?*

*Day 5*

Today you are Mary, listening to Jesus speak with your efficient, organized, hardworking sister. See his gentle touch as he embraces her, comforting her in her weariness.

Hear Jesus speak the essence of the abundant life. He does not discount the need for caring for the practical details of life, nor does he scold Martha or put her down. He doesn't deny the importance of what she has been doing. He knows, though, that she's not at peace.

Jesus yearns for your sister to experience the joy and peace of communion with him. When that is in place, all the other details of her life will work themselves into proper priority. He never forces his point of view on her but offers it to her with all the love of his heart. What she does with it is entirely up to her.

Now Jesus looks into your eyes. He reaches out and draws both you and Martha into the circle of his love. Imagine how it feels to stand in Jesus' embrace with your loved one. Feel his tender love for both of you healing the brokenness between you.

*Picture yourself with someone*
*with whom you need to make amends.*

*Who needs to be brought into the circle*
*of Christ's healing, forgiving love with you?*

# *Day 6*

Now you are Martha, the hardworking, efficient sister. Remember the times you have carried the load for the rest of the family and felt overburdened for being the responsible one. Think back over the long years of the same family patterns. Feel the resentment of doing for others what they should be doing for themselves. Think about how much you have relied on being good and reliable.

As you stand with Jesus and your sister, you want Jesus to chastise Mary for not helping you with the meal preparation. You would like an opportunity to tell of the many times Mary has shirked her responsibilities. As Jesus continues to speak, you can hardly believe your ears. He's telling you that Mary has done the right thing. Jesus says that your sister has "chosen the good part, *which will not be taken from her*" (v. 42, italics mine). How do you feel about that?

You recall hearing Jesus tell some of the other disciples that they should seek him first. You know there must be something to what he is saying, but for you to do that would mean turning all your values and your schedule upside down! You aren't sure you can change that much.

*Have you relied on your ability to be good enough
to bring you what you want?*

*How do your priorities need to change?*

*Allow the Living Christ to rearrange your priorities.*

*Let him show you the most important things.*

*Day 7*

The scene changes after dinner. You, as Mary, go to your room to retire for the evening. You sit by the open window of your room, gazing out at the star-studded sky. Smell the night smells and hear the crickets' persistent chirping. Feel the gentle, cool breeze brush your face and body.

The house is silent now, and you replay all the events of the day. You recall exactly how it felt to sit at the feet of Jesus, and you blush at the memory of Martha's public scolding, but you cannot be angry with her. You understand her need better now than you ever did before.

"It was worth it!" your heart cries in the night. It was worth any price you had to pay to hear the voice of Jesus and to sit in his presence. It was worth anything you had to do to be with him. If you had to do it all over again, you would risk Martha's rebuke or the reactions of others to sit in the presence of Jesus.

*How much do you want an unbroken,*
*unhindered fellowship with the Living Christ?*

*Are you willing to give up*
*your pride,*
*independence,*
*and rights*
*to be with Jesus moment by moment?*

*What is he asking of you?*

# Deliverance

MARK 5:1-20

## Day 1

The setting for this week's meditations is a lake in the region of the Gerasenes. Picture yourself as one of the disciples who is crossing the lake with Jesus. When you get out of the boat and begin to walk on the shore, a man "with an evil spirit" comes toward you. He is agitated and disheveled. As you look into his eyes, you see his confusion and desperation. You notice the offensive odor about him, hear the distorted sounds coming from his mouth, and are aware of his agony.

Others around you are making fun of the man. Hear someone mimic him. A local person explains to you that the man has been possessed with an unclean spirit for a long time and lives in the tombs. Everyone talks about the man as if he cannot hear what they are saying; but when you look in his eyes, you see that he knows how they feel about him.

What are your feelings about this man? Do you, too, turn aside in revulsion? Do you try to get Jesus to move away from him? Or do you look at him with compassion and identify with his suffering? Watch Jesus, calm and collected, standing firm as the man approaches him. There is something about Jesus' confidence and poise in the midst of chaos that calms you. Notice Jesus' gentle demeanor.

*Is there an outcast in your life?*

*How do you respond to him or her?*

## *Day 2*

Can you put yourself in the place of the demon-possessed man? Imagine that you are this tormented man, moving out of the tombs. You walk through the crowd of people, and everyone pulls back, far away from you. You see a woman turn away and pull her veil up around her face; a father draws his children out of the pathway, covering their eyes so that they won't "catch" your problem. You feel the shame and guilt. If they only knew your anguish, you say to yourself, they would understand.

See yourself walking steadfastly toward Jesus who is standing at the shore. There is something you notice about him that draws you to him. What is it that pulls you toward Jesus? Who is it that might try to shield Jesus from you? Who is it that keeps you moving toward Jesus, regardless of the reactions around you?

*There may be "tombs" in your life
that inhibit your joy in the present.*

*Are you clinging to problems or blessings from that past,
robbing yourself of the creativity of the present moment?*

*Are you bound by something that happened in the past
that you need to release to the redemptive hands of Christ?*

*Are you in bondage to your old self?*

*In what ways are you kept from a relationship with Jesus?*

*Is there anyone whose way to Jesus you are blocking?*

*Day 8*

Move in your imagination to the character of one of the townspeople. All of your life you have known the man they call "the demoniac." You have come to accept who he is and not worry about him.

You are walking toward the lakeshore where Jesus is. What you have heard about Jesus has piqued your curiosity. As you approach, you see that the man they call "the demoniac" has moved right up into Jesus' face and is shouting his agony at the teacher. You are horrified that he's one of the first to greet this important visitor—if he doesn't give a good impression of your town!

You try to rush toward Jesus to explain and to divert his attention to something more palatable. However, the crowd becomes more dense as you get closer. Finally, you speak to one of Jesus' assistants; surely he can get word to Jesus that he doesn't need to waste his time with a demoniac. The demoniac isn't going to change!

Hear yourself explaining to Jesus' assistant that many have tried to bind the demoniac, but to no avail. Tell him all the ways you have tried to force the demoniac to change. Describe the times you or others have tried to chain him.

*What things or people have you tried to change by force?*

*What aspects of your life have you sought to control*
*by imposing your will or your human strength?*

*Has it really worked?*

# Day 4

Once again become the demoniac, identifying with his appearance, his behavior, his agony. Look down and observe the scars and scabs on your arms and legs where, in your anguish, you have gashed yourself. See the open wounds and feel the pain you have inflicted on yourself.

As you stand before Jesus, you have a vague awareness of your years in the tombs. You recall your self-imposed punishment. You remember times you have tried to free or heal yourself, only to be plunged deeper into self-recrimination and failure. Your guilt and shame, your terrifying thoughts and crippling emotions, have bound you as surely as if you were in prison, bound by literal chains and beaten by actual guards.

*In the silence of prayer,*
*recall those areas of your life*
*where you are bound by your own choices.*

*Think about those self-inflicted punishments.*

*Tell Jesus all the ways you have hurt yourself,*
*everything you have done that has kept you bound*
*in pain and punishment.*

*What does he say to you about the pain*
*you have inflicted on yourself?*

*How does he look at you?*

*What do you feel,*
*standing in the very presence of Grace?*

# Day 5

What is your name?" Jesus asks you, the demoniac, as you stand before him at the lake.

"My name is Legion," you tell him, and he knows you are talking about the many persons in you, each clamoring for attention.

Jesus understands that part of you is sane and part is insane. He knows and accepts that you are at the same time mature and childish. He knows you long for wholeness and responsibility while the unclean spirits want to stay fragmented and irresponsible. Jesus is acquainted with the real you, however diminished, that is noble, generous, honest, and fine. He can separate those qualities from the base, selfish, devious, and narcissistic characteristics of the demons. He knows that you are self-destructive and self-protective, all at the same time. Jesus understands ambivalence.

Into the anarchy of conflicting desires and the tyranny of a fragmented self, Jesus Christ can bring order and harmony. He can heal the total self so that a person's thoughts, feelings, actions, and desires are centered in his love and power and are all moving in the same direction.

In the presence of Jesus, there is peace of mind because Jesus brings a new orientation and a new affection. As the kingdom of God comes to rule in a mind and in the emotions, there is a new power and soundness of mind. Fear leaves in the presence of Christ, and love emerges.

*Ask Christ*
*to heal your fragmented life*
*and give you peace.*

# Day 6

As you, the demoniac, stand in the presence of Christ, forget that anyone else is there. Feel the warm sand on your bare feet. Look at the fabric of Jesus' clothing; see his features. Notice especially the gentle, accepting look in his eyes. Feel the breeze on your wounds. Time stands so still that you can almost feel your heart beating.

All your life people have avoided you, but this man Jesus stands there before you. He even touches you, and as he does, something new courses through you. Is that life you feel in your dead body?

Your mind, which has raced from one thing to another and back in a ceaseless, obsessive whirling maelstrom, is suddenly calm. Your entire focus is on Jesus who looks past the absurdity of your behavior to the pain at the core of your being.

For the first time in your life, you feel accepted. Jesus is the first one who has treated you like a person instead of a problem. He doesn't try to change you by berating or criticizing you. He doesn't try to control you with the chains of opinion. Jesus simply loves you, and you feel that love move through your craziness down deep into your soul.

*Imagine Jesus,*
*looking at you with the eyes of acceptance.*

# Day 7

You are a town leader, a herdsman, watching the scene at the shore between Jesus and the town's "problem" inhabitant. Before your astonished eyes, the pigs on the hillside—your pigs—suddenly turn wild and run down the slope into the sea! What did Jesus do? The man who was spirit-possessed now seems normal. Doesn't Jesus know that he may have healed the demoniac but ruined your livelihood?

You run up to Jesus, wildly accusing him of destroying your life. You are vaguely aware that your actions are as bizarre as the demoniac's used to be, but you have an excuse! Jesus has brought devastation to your household, and he did it just to heal somebody who wasn't worth anything! How does Jesus respond to your accusations? How do you feel, watching your herd run down into the sea? What do you do?

You are aware of the irony: The health and wholeness of the former demoniac has upset you more than his sickness because his healing has impacted your personal welfare. That is far more important to you than his well-being. Admit to yourself that as much as the demoniac embarrassed you, your own personal welfare is more important to you.

*Are you willing for Christ to make others well,*
*even if it means your life is unsettled?*

*Are there ways that you order Jesus*
*not to interfere in your life?*

# Who Is Jesus, Anyway?

MATTHEW 16:13-20

# *Day 1*

How would it feel to be in the "inner circle" of Jesus' friends? Would you want that kind of association and the responsibility that went with it? Would you like being entrusted with Jesus' deepest thoughts and hardest teachings?

As you move into the silence of today's meditation, picture yourself sitting with Jesus and the other members of the inner circle of friends. All of you have just come from an encounter with the Pharisees and Sadducees and are discussing with Jesus the way the Jewish leaders demanded a sign from him to prove who he is.

Imagine that you twelve are seated around Jesus. See the buildings of Caesarea Philippi in the distance. Hear the song of a bird across the way and feel the earth beneath you as you recline against a small tree. Look closely at each disciple and then into the face of Jesus. Recall how well he handled his questioners.

"Who do they say that I am?" he asks the group.

*You have heard various evaluations of Jesus:*
*a myth,*
*a prophet,*
*a good man,*
*a moral purist,*
*the Son of God,*
*the greatest teacher who ever lived.*

*In the quietness,*
*think about your perception of Jesus.*

*Is your judgment based on*
*fact, prejudice, or experience?*

## Day 2

As you sit in the circle with the other disciples, listen to their answers to Jesus' question, "Who do others say that I am?" Imagine the disciples all talking at once. Jesus searches their faces as they grapple with his identity and purpose.

You hear one of the disciples answer, "They say you are Elijah," and another, "Some say you are Jeremiah."

You know that your friends want to impress on Jesus that people think he's important, like the prophets.

You look at Jesus, scanning his face for some sense of how he regards their answers. Deep within you is a growing restlessness, a turmoil of mind and spirit, giving birth to new understanding. There is the darkness of unknowing that precedes the light of knowing.

Jesus looks at you for an answer. You are unsure of what to say, but you know that no matter how great a compliment it is to compare Jesus with the prophets, their greatness doesn't compare with his.

Jesus is a great puzzle. He is godly, yet so human. He is sovereign, but neighborly, sitting here with all of you. He is intense, but tranquil; he is mysterious and transparent; demanding, but forgiving. Jesus is majestic, but vulnerable.

*In the silence,*
*simply be with Jesus*
*and let him speak.*

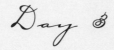

# Day 8

Return in your imagination to the scene with the disciples. You are in the middle of a discussion about Jesus' identity, trying to sort through your own thoughts to an answer that is not only right but sufficient.

Think about all the reasons you have chosen to follow Jesus. Make a mental list of all you want Jesus to be for you.

Do you want him to be your personal bodyguard, protecting you from life? Would you like him to be your own special cosmic bellboy, meeting your list of demands and desires on your timetable? Is Jesus your insurance policy, guaranteeing that you won't burn in a fiery hell? Is he a custom for you or a conviction? Is he the object of a periodic festival or the object of your deepest devotion?

Do you want Jesus to be a benevolent grandfather, looking past your faults and errors? Or would you prefer a Santa Claus who will bestow magical gifts and favors on you at appropriate times? Is Jesus your amulet, warding off evil spirits?

You are trying to be honest with yourself, searching your heart and mind for your true motivation for hanging around with Jesus.

*Jesus knows the truth about your heart.*
*Do you?*

# Day 4

Today, you are Peter in the circle of Jesus' disciples. You are sitting close to Jesus, listening intently to the lively discussion. You watch Jesus as he looks at each of your friends. Finally, he turns those penetrating eyes on you, and your heart races.

"What about you, Peter?" Jesus asks. "Who do you say that I am?"

You are keenly aware of the silence that falls on the group. Though you've never really discussed it before, everyone knows how important the answer is. It really does matter who Jesus is to you.

Jesus can no longer be a theory to be discussed or an argument to be debated. Your intellectual grappling won't meet the demand of the moment. No longer can you simply go along with the group, resting on others' opinions of who Jesus is. Traditions and your heritage won't help you now.

You search your mind for the "right" answer to Jesus' question. You start to ask him if it really matters, but the look in his eyes stops you. It is the moment to decide who Jesus is.

*If Jesus were to walk up to you*
*right this moment and ask you,*
*"Who do you say that I am?"*
*what would your answer be?*

## *Day 5*

Return in your imagination to that emotion-charged moment when Jesus asks Peter to declare his understanding of who Jesus is. As you, Peter, face Jesus and his question, there is no doubt. You know who he is. The answer that would not come from your mind has sprung from your heart. Though you cannot rationalize your answer, you know with a certainty that cannot be shaken that this man Jesus is the Christ, the Son of the Living God.

Hear your voice as you make your declaration to Jesus. Are your words clear and distinct? Do you speak boldly and with confidence and conviction? Does the joy of knowing spill out of your heart and into your words?

You clearly affirm to Jesus that you know who he is. Then you watch his expression. Do his eyes lock yours in a bond of communion? Does he smile at you? Do tears of joy come to his eyes when he realizes that someone in his group "gets it"?

Imagine the joy of Jesus when one of his children recognizes who he is. Imagine his delight when one of his own moves beyond mere mental assent to true belief and total commitment to him. Think about his love when one of his chosen ones gives up the debates and decides to follow him.

*Can you stand before Christ and make Peter's confession?*

*Is Peter's affirmation yours?*

# *Day 6*

As Peter, you have declared a knowledge of Christ that is beyond human reason and logic. As you sit there in the wonder of knowing, Jesus speaks to you. He says that God revealed this to you. That makes sense because you know it didn't come from your own reasoning. Being able to accept Christ for who he is, is itself a gift of grace.

You have done something that is unusual for you, and you wonder if your friends notice that you are acting out of character. With your practical orientation, you have made a leap of faith that makes no common sense; but that doesn't matter because the power set free in you is like nothing you could ever have imagined. It is as if choosing to believe empowers you to see.

With your gaze fixed on Jesus, you know that after this moment, your life will never be the same. Although Jesus has not explained it to you, you realize that acknowledging him is both exhilarating and burdensome. In knowing Jesus as Lord, you are set free; but with that freedom comes a terrific responsibility. You know that the others sense something significant has happened between you and Jesus. You wonder if they, too, now recognize who he is.

*In the silence,*
*see yourself before Christ,*
*acknowledging him as Lord and Savior,*
*Son of the Living God.*

*Day 7*

In that circle of disciples, you, as Peter, are across from Jesus. The other disciples move toward him. It is as if they, too, want to be drawn into the dynamic force that dances between Jesus and Peter.

Hear Jesus acknowledge that you understand who he is. See Jesus throw back his head with the joy of being understood. Hear his laughter as he celebrates a new depth of relationship with one of his chosen ones.

As the laughter ebbs, Jesus' expression becomes serious as he looks at you and tells you that because you have understood, you will be given great responsibility. Jesus begins to describe a new kingdom, and he wants you to help get it started.

You protest and start listing your faults, but Jesus quiets you and tells you that his way is best. You protest that you are weak, and he tells you that his choice is to take weak people and make them strong as they follow him. Jesus says you will be the first stone in the new edifice of the "church"; you tell him you don't know what that is. Jesus tells you that he will be the head of this church, and that you will help him build it with people who, like you, discover who he is. Jesus explains that he is entrusting his work to you because you know who he is, and that you will open the door to thousands.

*What part does Christ want you
to play in his kingdom?*

# Neither Do I Condemn You

JOHN 8:1-11

# *Day 1*

Imagine that you are a woman living in Jesus' time. One day, when you are with a lover, a group of Pharisees and teachers of the law burst into your room.

In the confusion of the moment, terror strikes your heart. You fear that they are taking you out to stone you. The man who has just professed his devotion to you disappears as some of the young men you know very well grab you and drag you out into the sunlight.

You scream as you feel their rough hands on your body. Experience your terror as they drag you through the street and throw you down in the dirt. You hear their mocking voices, and you'd like to remind them what you know about them, but you dare not speak for fear of further violence. You won't even look up to see your accusers' faces.

You hear those who have sought your favors telling somebody how they have caught you in the very act of adultery. They are yelling insults and threats as they describe your crime. Your body shudders with fear. The scratches on your face and arms begin to sting. Quietly, you spit the dirt out of your mouth.

*In the silence of your safe place,*
*imagine how it would be*
*to be caught and exposed*
*as a soiled plaything of men.*

*Think about how it feels to be judged.*

*How do you judge and accuse others?*

# *Day 2*

In your imagination, recreate the scene of yesterday. Hear the shouts of your accusers. Taste the dust, mingled with your tears and the blood from your wounds. You know what the law demands. Now you weep silently for yourself and your wasted life. You pray for strength to face your punishment; you do not beg for mercy but accept the inevitable pain and shame.

You are vaguely aware that the person your accusers have brought you to has stooped down to the ground beside you. You wait to hear his verdict; instead, you hear a scraping on the ground. He's writing on the ground with his finger. Then you hear him say, "He who is without sin among you, let him be the first to throw a stone at her." You hold your breath and barely turn your head to look in his direction.

There is silence, an unbelievable, eerie silence. You hear feet shuffling, and you raise your head. The man is looking straight into your eyes, and you feel as if you are looking into the eyes of pure holiness and love. You have never experienced compassion in all your life, but you know that this is it.

*Christ is looking at you with utter mercy and love.*

*How does it feel?*

## Day 8

Return to the scene of yesterday, beginning in the room of the woman caught in adultery. This time imagine that you are a Pharisee, an older man who has upheld the letter of the law, at least publicly.

You have been talking with the other Pharisees about this man, Jesus, and the more you think about how he is disrupting your community, the angrier you get. Someone suggests a plot for catching Jesus in his own arguments; the enthusiasm for the plot grows, and the voices get louder. Somehow, you are swept along to the room of the woman you know well.

You stand back and let the younger men forge ahead. Something you cannot name keeps you from laying a hand on her. Nevertheless, you participate in the mob's action, following the raucous group out into the presence of Jesus.

You look around, hoping you won't be noticed. You hear the mob's accusations, but you don't look at the woman or at Jesus.

When you hear Jesus say, "If anyone is without sin, let him cast the first stone," an icy terror fills your heart. More mellow than the young zealots yelling in Jesus' face, you know that your judgment of this woman judges you. The gentleness of age seeps up through your judging, and you turn away in shame.

*Allow the Spirit of Christ*
*to reveal your harsh and critical spirit.*

*Let him show you your own sin;*
*it is the way to freedom.*

# Day 4

Go once again to the room of the woman caught in adultery. This time, you are a young Pharisee, filled with the vitality and zeal for the law.

This man Jesus is threatening everything you hold dear! What must you do but protect the law? How could you look your rabbi in the eye if you didn't defend his teaching? Why, your father himself would die in shame if he knew that you didn't come to the defense of the faith! What better way to do it than to use the woman of ill repute to trick Jesus?

You charge through the streets, moving straight to the woman's house with a familiarity you won't admit even to yourself. You rip the curtain from the doorway and storm into her room, shamelessly throwing aside the covers and seizing her roughly. You don't even see the man who is with her.

She calls you by name, but you ignore her. Your friend comes to your aid, helping you drag her through the room and out into the sunlight. You have no mercy; all that counts is trapping Jesus, and you don't care whom you have to hurt to do that.

When you hear Jesus' words, "If anyone is without sin, let him cast the first stone," a vile rage boils up through your body. You seethe with self-righteousness. How dare Jesus turn the focus of condemnation away from this filthy woman.

*Ask the Spirit of Truth to lead you into the truth about your own judgmentalism and self-righteousness.*

*He will set you free.*

# Day 5

As you enter your time of creative prayer today, let your imagination recreate the sounds and sights of yesterday's violence. Recall Jesus' penetrating question to the accusers. See yourself as the woman, looking into the merciful eyes of God.

"Where are your accusers?" the man asks you.

Slowly, painfully, you lift yourself up on your elbow. Through swollen eyes, you look around you and then back at Jesus. Only the two of you remain.

You are looking into the face of utter holiness and purity. With all your brokenness, you are gazing into the eyes of the one who is whole, perfect, and without blemish. In his presence, you know too well the sordid stains of your blemished life. You should probably be afraid, but you are not.

"They aren't here," you tell him weakly, and then you hear him say that he doesn't condemn you either.

Time stands still for you as you ponder what it means for this man to withhold condemnation. For the first time in your life, you experience forgiveness. He isn't merely excusing you. This is no light or flippant act of smoothing things over. It is as if this man reaches into your heart and heals your deepest wound.

*In the silence,*
*recall your brokenness.*

*Admit your sin to Christ.*

*Then hear him say,*
*"You are forgiven."*

# *Day 6*

As you ponder the scene of this week's meditation, hear again Jesus' words to you, the woman caught in adultery.

"Neither do I condemn you," he says, and time stands still.

You don't know what it means to be forgiven instead of condemned. It is beyond your wildest thoughts how you will live if you are forgiven, if you are free of the past.

As you pull yourself to your feet, you stand between the past and the future, filled with many feelings. You are grateful that you are still alive, but you don't know what to do next. You feel the grace and mercy wash over your soiled past. How will you live the days of your future if you accept this? What will your accusers do if you change? Are you strong enough to be free?

And then Jesus gives you the key for the future. "Don't do what you were doing anymore," he tells you.

Is it possible to just stop that self-defeating behavior? Can you quit going in one direction and now go in another, healthier direction? Can you choose to be different?

*As you sit in the silence,*
*ask the Living Christ to reveal to you*
*what you need to stop doing.*

*Ask him to show you*
*what you need to begin doing*
*to express the mercy he has given you.*

*Ask him for the strength and courage*
*to live in freedom and grace.*

# Day 7

As you enter into your meditation time today, get in touch with your feminine self. The part of you that is open, vulnerable, adaptive, and sensitive is the feminine, whether you are a man or a woman. Each person has a feminine self that is giving, gentle, dependent, warm, and nurturing—whether or not those traits are expressed or even recognized.

Think of the times you have given authority over yourself to someone other than Christ. Allow the Spirit of Christ to show you the ways you have sold out to others, letting them make decisions that only you should make.

Remember a time when you allowed yourself to become vulnerable to another and were hurt. Bring to your awareness occasions when you were sensitive and gentle, and someone took advantage of you. Allow yourself to recall when you misused your feminine strengths in relationships to manipulate others or to gain power over them.

You also may have had experiences when someone attacked or violated you, using the masculine strengths of dominance, aggression, power, or competitiveness. You may have been wounded by someone, either male or female, who misused the masculine strength of independence or authority with you.

*See the Spirit of Christ reaching down*
*to your feminine self.*

*Hear him tell you*
*that you have been healed*
*to be your full self.*

# Healing Your Inner Child

MATTHEW 19:13-15

## Day 1

For a pleasant interlude in your day, draw apart to a grassy hillside. See Jesus mingling with a crowd of people in the sunlight. Hear the laughter of children and the easy banter among friends.

Imagine that you are a parent walking through the crowd hand in hand with your child. Watch yourself slowing your steps to accommodate the child. Now and then, look down and notice your child's innocence, and feel your heart fill with love.

As you walk together toward Jesus, you marvel at the trust your child has in you. The child doesn't ask where you are taking him, but follows you gladly and willingly. You remember when you trusted that easily.

From your neighbors you have heard stories about this rabbi's ability to heal people and perform miracles. He does amazing things, and you want him to place his hands on your child's head to give him a blessing.

Moving closer, you see that there are already plenty of children crowded around Jesus. He is beaming down at each one, touching them gently. It is as if he "sparkles" on the children, and they can't get close enough to him.

*In the silence,*
*bring your inner child to Jesus.*

# Day 2

Today, take on the person of a disciple who is with Jesus, mingling among the people. You have seen Jesus heal the sick, listen to the troubled, and comfort the bereaved. You have watched as he performed miracles, and you have heard him teach.

As his close friend, you feel a sense of responsibility toward Jesus. After all, someone has to look after him! Who knows better than you how costly his ministry is to him? Who can tell more than you when he is weary and needs a break from the incessant demands of the crowd?

You watch as the crowd builds around Jesus, and your concern for him deepens. A child breaks away from his parent and runs up to Jesus. See Jesus bend over and pick up the child, swinging the youngster high into the air and laughing with delight!

Are you shocked when Jesus acts with spontaneity and is utterly devoid of self-consciousness in the presence of the children? Do you worry about their wearing him out, or do you enjoy seeing Jesus with the children?

Suddenly, many children rush toward Jesus, pulling on him and begging for attention. Finally, he sits down, and they scramble up onto his lap. Your concern moves you to rush over and intervene. You scold the parents for letting the children run loose.

*How does the adult in you*
*keep your inner child from coming freely*
*into the presence of Christ?*

*Day 3*

As you move in your creative imagery to reconstruct the meditation of this week, become the little child whose mother has brought you to the hillside to see Jesus.

Feel your hand in your mother's as you walk across the grassy slope. Stop to pick a wildflower and hear your mother hurry you on. Feel her pull your arm. Notice your sandals on the grass. Hear a baby babbling in its mother's arms.

It feels so good to be out in the fresh air, out under the open sky. You begin to skip to keep up with your mother. You feel as free as a bird.

The crowd becomes thicker as you skip across the grass, struggling to keep up with your mother. Suddenly someone steps on your toe, and you want to cry, but then you catch a glimpse of a man who has children climbing all over him. He is laughing and teasing the children, and there is something about the way he looks at each one that makes you want to be close to him.

"This is Jesus, the man who will give you a blessing," your mother tells you, and you look straight into his face.

Acting on some inner impulse, you let go of your mother's hand and move up close to Jesus. He looks down into your face and smiles at you.

*Recall yourself as a little child.*

*Sit with Jesus in the sun.*

*Savor that feeling of being loved completely by him.*

# Day 4

Again, today, you are a child, standing close to Jesus. In your imagination, recall the scene as you played it yesterday.

As you stand near Jesus, you lean against him. You have never felt such joy before! What a nice man he is. He has such a kind voice.

Jesus feels your presence at his knee and asks you if you would like to sit on his lap. You look at your mother, and she nods her approval.

Jesus gently lifts you up to his lap, and even though a child is sitting on his other knee, you feel like you are the most important person in the world. You feel so welcome, as if Jesus really wants you to be with him.

You have heard your parents talk about feeling special, and now you know what that means. Even though you may not be able to say how you feel, you sense that you are precious to Jesus. When he embraces you with those strong arms, you feel protected and loved. You know that you are valuable to him.

You hear some adults talking in the background, and then you hear Jesus tell them to let the children come to him. You don't know what that means, but you notice that the adults don't say anything else.

When you are ready, Jesus puts you down on the ground and places his hands on your head.

*How does it feel to be blessed by Jesus?*

## Day 5

Return to the scene of this week's meditation as the mother who has brought her child to Jesus. As your child breaks away from you, you are startled. At first, you are concerned about losing sight of your child, and then about how your child will feel away from you.

Quickly, though, you lose all concern, for you see the way Jesus welcomes your child. Besides, your child is intrigued with Jesus, just as you are.

As you watch Jesus lift your child to his lap, you catch your breath. Maybe Jesus will give your child a special blessing! Perhaps just by being in his presence, your child might grow up to be like Jesus! Surely, this is an important moment. Tears trickle down your cheeks.

You stand there watching your child, but your memory offers up pictures of you as a little child. You remember how it felt to be small and vulnerable, dependent and trusting. Where did that little child in you go when you became an adult?

You wish you had the courage to walk right up to Jesus like your child did and ask him to bless you. It feels as if the little child in you still needs his blessing. You wish you could sit on Jesus' lap and feel that safety and security.

*How can the adult part of you
bring your inner child to Jesus?*

*Hear Jesus say,
it is never too late to be a child.*

## Day 6

Once again, assume the persona of the disciple with the self-imposed responsibility of protecting Jesus. It is up to you to make sure the crowds don't wear him out. It is your task to provide his food and get him to a place of rest when he is weary.

As you watch the children forcing their way to Jesus, you become alarmed and speak up, scolding the parents for not being more careful. Hear the harshness in your voice and feel the tightness in your face and neck. Things aren't going as you had planned; besides, you are tired too, from being so responsible.

Over the din of the children's laughter, Jesus' voice pierces your consciousness. As you realize that you are being scolded, you blush with embarrassment. You don't like making a mistake, especially in public.

"Don't keep the children from coming to me," Jesus says to you. "Don't hold them back, for it is such as these who will enter the kingdom of heaven."

What is Jesus talking about? Does he mean that children are the ones who understand best? Is it children who most easily connect with Jesus, after all?

Watching Jesus, you notice there is something special going on between him and the children.

*Ask the Spirit of Christ to reveal to you*
*what it would mean for you to become as a little child.*

# Day 7

In the final scene on the hillside, you, as a little child, hop down from the lap of Jesus and run to your mother. You want to tell her what it was like to be that close to Jesus, but you can't explain it.

All you know is that you have received a blessing from someone who isn't like anybody else you know. You feel happy and contented, and you like yourself. You want to return again tomorrow to sit with Jesus on the hillside.

Over and over, Jesus told his disciples that the requirements for entering the kingdom of God were different from those for being part of an earthly kingdom. He turned the values of the society upside down and told the disciples that instead of becoming powerful and important, they must become childlike.

Becoming childlike means being open and trusting, receptive and pliable. It means retaining a beginner's mind and a teachable spirit. The childlike, who are willing to lay down pride and to say that they do not know, will understand the truth of life in Christ.

In the silence, call up the memory of yourself as a child. Remember what it was like to be dependent, before life forced you into the mold of an adult.

*That little child is still within you.*

*Allow Christ to bless your child.*

*Then let that little child teach you how to live.*

# Turning Point

LUKE 19:1-10

# Day 1

Picture yourself as a rich and successful tax collector from the town of Jericho. Your name is Zacchaeus, and you have worked hard to be where you are.

Think back on the long hours you have put in to "arrive." Recall the personal sacrifices you have made so that your family can live in comfort. Remember the deals you have struck and the rules you have stretched for your benefit so you could enjoy the standard of living of the successful.

On this day, however, the constant ostracism by your fellow citizens has finally caught up with you. You are tired of people avoiding you when they pass you in the streets. You are weary of seeing people look the other way when you try to speak to them. Most of all, a queasy guilt nags at your conscience; you know you have worked things to your advantage all along, and you don't feel good about yourself.

For some reason you can't explain, you have a hunger that your acquisitions don't appease. There is an emptiness in having it all. People look at you and think you have it made. If only they knew the aching pain you carry around; if only they knew how lonely you are.

*In the silence,*
*ask God to reveal the ways you have tried*
*to fill your inner hunger with achievement and success.*

# Day 2

As Zacchaeus, move away from your desk, rubbing your forehead in weariness. You don't know why the fatigue won't go away; you get enough rest, but somehow life has gone flat for you. You just don't get that thrill out of cutting a deal anymore.

See yourself moving out into the street. You shield your eyes from the sunlight that contrasts sharply with your dark office. You notice that the crowd around the square is bigger and noisier than usual, and you walk toward the center of excitement.

"Jesus, come this way!" someone shouts, and you turn around to see your neighbor beckoning to a man. You have heard stories about Jesus, but you know he is merely a carpenter, and so you haven't paid much attention.

"Jesus! Jesus! Jesus!" Over and over the voices call his name, and for some reason you can't explain, you linger in the street, waiting to see what will happen. The crowd pushes and shoves around you, and because you are short, you can't see. You break away from the crowd and run ahead to a sycamore tree. The only way you will see Jesus is to climb up into the tree.

It's a pretty ordinary setting for a life-changing encounter. A street in your hometown. A common tree. Who would think that the extraordinary might break through here on a workday?

*Wherever you are,*
*Christ is.*

*No matter how plain your circumstances,*
*he can change your life.*

*Day 3*

As Zacchaeus, you stand at the foot of the sycamore tree, about to climb up into the safety of its limbs. Your shortness has been a problem all your life, but today it may turn out to be an advantage. You can get up above the crowd and see better than anyone else!

You tell yourself that it may look pretty weird for you, a grown man, to climb up into the boughs of a tree, but you want to see Jesus enough to take the risk of ridicule. There is something about him that draws you. You can't explain it, but for the first time in a long time, a person has made you curious enough to lay down your defenses and get outside your self-protective shell.

As you grab the bough closest to you, you tell yourself that what everybody thinks doesn't matter anyway. Nobody likes you, and they talk about you all the time. You have grown accustomed to being the town outcast. What difference will it make if you try to see Jesus from the top of a tree? At least you are away from the people!

See yourself climb the sycamore tree until you find a place in its protective arms from which you can watch the scene beneath you. Feel the roughness of the bark against your skin. Feel yourself balancing so that you won't fall.

*What imperfection or defect do you carry?*

*What are you willing to give up in order to see Jesus?*

## Day 4

In your imagination, recreate the scene of yourself as Zacchaeus in the sycamore tree. The throngs of people beneath you are scurrying about, trying to get close to Jesus. Smile to yourself because you have the best viewing spot of all!

You wonder what is so compelling about Jesus that people can't stay away from him. Is it the way he takes time to notice each person? Is it the vibrancy that dances in his face when he smiles? You notice the way he touches people, gently and firmly; you watch his concern for the sick and the lame.

From your seat in the tree, you feel a power in Jesus that you haven't seen in another human being. You remember when power was the one thing you thought you had to have to be happy; now you have power, and it isn't what you want. You are aware that the power Jesus manifests is different from what you have.

Suddenly, Jesus stops beneath your tree and looks up into your face. How did he know you were there? You should feel embarrassed at being found up in a tree, but you don't.

Then Jesus calls you by name and goes on to do the unthinkable. He invites himself to your house, in front of everyone.

*See Jesus walk right up to you*
*wherever you are today*
*and call you by name.*

*Hear him tell you*
*he wants to go home with you.*

*Day 5*

There are moments when Jesus comes to a person with the message of a new beginning and of hope. He says, "Your past is forgiven. I'm going to transform your present. And I'm going to redirect your future." It is a fortunate person, indeed, who recognizes the turning point.

See yourself again as Zacchaeus. As you climb down from the sycamore tree, your heart is beating wildly. All the guilt you have carried for years seems to lift in Jesus' presence. No longer does it take courage for you to mingle with the crowd; with Jesus, you stand tall and brave.

Can it really be that he wants to go home with you? What is it that makes this man willing to go where your colleagues and cohorts wouldn't dare to go? You notice not only that Jesus has no shame or embarrassment about being with you, but also that he seems to like you!

See yourself walking down the streets of Jericho to your home. Hear yourself calling to your servants to bring refreshments. Notice the censure of people along the route, but realize that it doesn't matter. You are so happy to be the host of Jesus that you don't care what they think.

See yourself ushering Jesus to the place of honor in your home.

*Jesus wants to be at home with you.*

*Will you let him?*

# Day 6

Today, use your creative imagination to reconstruct the street scene in Jericho. Assume the persona of an onlooker, a respectable leader of the town. You, too, have hurried through the streets, hoping to get a glimpse of Jesus. You know that when he sees you, he will certainly give you a blessing!

When you arrive at the main street, you are out of breath. You pause to collect yourself, searching the crowd for Jesus. You have seen him before, but you didn't pay much attention to him until you heard about all the things he was doing for your neighbors.

There he is! That must be Jesus! Or, is it? He couldn't be with Zacchaeus, could he? A man like Jesus wouldn't risk his reputation to talk to someone like that crook, at least not out in broad daylight!

Your mouth falls open in utter shock and horror as you watch Jesus move with Zacchaeus toward Zacchaeus' home! Before your eyes, Jesus goes right through the door into that house where you wouldn't be caught dead!

You shake your head. A friend walks over to you, and the two of you can't quit talking about what you have just seen. Maybe this Jesus isn't who you thought he was.

*In the silence,*
*allow the Spirit of Christ to reveal*
*your self-righteousness and judgmentalism.*

# Day 17

Return to the interior of Zacchaeus' home where you are the host welcoming Jesus to your home. Where do you have Jesus sit?

Be aware of the feelings stirring inside of you. You know that a divine disturbance and a holy discontent have brought you to this place of encounter. You know, even though you don't know how you know, that Jesus has answers for you. He found you and called you by name.

Hear yourself confessing your sin to Jesus. Feel the relief as your pent-up feelings and regrets, your stifled longings and yearnings, find expression in a torrent of words. Watch Jesus' face as you tell him all about your life; see the compassion and empathy when you say that you want to live a new way.

You pause, thinking how a good host would let the guest speak. You ask yourself why Jesus chose you for his guest appearance. Why me? I am not worthy! He should have gone to a priest's home!

Feel the grace of God wash over you as Jesus declares that salvation has come to you. You sit in your own home with Jesus, knowing that you have crossed a line and will never again be the same.

*In the silence,*
*allow the Living Christ to show you*
*who you can be if you give your whole self to him.*

# Come Forth!

JOHN 11:1-44

## Day 1

As you enter into this week's meditations, take the part of Martha, friend of Jesus. You have hosted Jesus many times in your home, and you know him well.

Your brother Lazarus is very ill, and because you are the eldest in the family, you assume responsibility for taking action.

When you and your sister discuss what to do, you immediately know you should contact Jesus, because he has the power to heal your brother. In good faith, you send the message to Jesus that his good friend Lazarus is sick.

Once you have dispatched the messenger, you return to sit by the bedside of your brother. You know there is nothing else you can do for him, but you have complete confidence that Jesus will come soon. You trust Jesus so much that you are willing to take your greatest problem to him and leave it in his hands.

*Moving your focus into your own personal life today, call to mind your loved ones.*

*Hear yourself telling Jesus how much you love each one.*

*Hear him tell you that he also loves them.*

*Now, hear yourself telling Jesus your greatest problem.*

*See yourself confidently entrusting him with that problem.*

# Day 2

As you return to the scene of a home where Jesus has spent many happy hours, you are Martha again. You have sent your message to Jesus, and now you are becoming impatient because he hasn't come.

See yourself pacing back and forth beside the bed of your brother. You pause long enough to wash his feverish brow with cool water. You try to get him to eat, but he refuses. Hear him groan.

The day drags on, and you become more and more anxious as you watch your brother's condition worsen. Now and then you walk over to the window and peer into the distance, hoping to see Jesus approaching. Hour after hour you wait.

Your sister, Mary, comes into the room and asks about Jesus. The two of you talk about the strange tardiness of your friend. Surely he would come if he knew how serious the situation was. Perhaps he didn't get the message. Maybe something happened on the way to your home; after all, he has been attacked more and more by the Pharisees.

The agony of waiting for Jesus wears on you, and you become more and more agitated. Maybe he doesn't care as much as you thought he did.

*Move your focus to your own personal waiting times.*

*Allow the Spirit of Christ to soothe your worried self.*

*Hear him tell you that he is always right on time.*

*Day 8*

You are Martha, friend of Jesus, and you have waited for hours for his coming. Now your brother has died, and you have prepared him for burial. It seems that your grief will overwhelm you, and you cannot understand why Jesus did not come to your aid.

Then you hear Jesus' voice, and you move out of your house toward him, searching for the right thing to say. Will it do any good to vent your anger? Do you dare ask him where he has been?

Jesus comes toward you, and you don't understand his calmness. You think surely he must not know that Lazarus has died. You can't keep from chastising him a bit; after all, if only he had been here, this wouldn't have happened!

Jesus does the strangest thing. Instead of comforting you in your grief, he begins to talk about resurrection and life and belief in him. This is no time for a philosophical discussion!

Still, something about the conversation comforts you and gives that confidence and hope you always feel when Jesus is with you. You don't understand why he delayed in meeting your need, but when you look into his face, you know that you trust him completely.

*Is there something in your life*
*that seems hopelessly finished?*

*Bring it to Christ.*

*Tell him how you feel about your loss.*

116

*Day 4*

For today's meditation, take the part of Mary, Martha's younger sister. You are the one who has sat at Jesus' feet time and again. Now you have waited through the long, dark hours with Martha, agonizing over the absence of Jesus.

You watched Lazarus suffer and saw Martha wring her hands and pace the floor in agony. Now that your beloved brother is dead, you are filled with confusion and grief. Why didn't Jesus come when he got word that Lazarus was sick?

As you sit in your home, various friends crowd around to comfort you, but nothing will ease the pain of your loss and confusion concerning Jesus' absence. You weep for yourself and for your family.

You are vaguely aware of conversations outside the house, and you hear Martha's voice quietly speaking with someone. Is it Jesus? You don't even bother to investigate.

Martha comes into the room and tells you that Jesus has come. You rush toward him, relief flooding your heart until you remember that it is too late. Lazarus is already dead! What can be done now? When you look up, you see through your tears that Jesus is with you.

*Imagine having Jesus present with you*
*in your sorrows even now.*

# Day 5

Imagine that you are a friend of the sisters who have lost their brother. You have come to weep with Mary and Martha and to help them with the many things that must be done.

You hear them talking about Jesus and how it would have been different if he had been there. You don't say anything, but something in you wants to tell them that it wouldn't have made any difference. You have been suspicious of Jesus all along, and his absence at this time has confirmed all your doubts. Mary and Martha shouldn't have relied on him so much; they set themselves up for disappointment.

When you hear the uproar outside the house and realize that it is because Jesus has come, you walk outside toward the sisters. Maybe somebody like you, a friend of the family, should protect them from this strange man, especially at a time when they are so vulnerable. You never can tell how people will take advantage of the bereaved.

The sound of Mary's weeping fills your heart with sorrow, and you move forward to comfort her.

Suddenly, you hear an anguished cry like none you have heard before. When you look up, you realize that it is Jesus who is weeping. Stunned, you watch as Jesus grieves.

*God grieved over the death of Lazarus.*

*God grieves for you, too, when you are hurting.*

*Do you believe that?*

# Day 6

You are Martha again, and you are walking with Jesus to Lazarus' tomb. See yourself holding Jesus' hand. You are hardly aware of others who are crowding around you; only Jesus matters in this moment of need.

All anger at Jesus for being late has dissipated. You have watched him weep for his friend, and now you only wish to comfort him. You think that Jesus simply wants to be near the tomb, and so you go with him, giving him support.

You cannot believe your ears when Jesus commands someone to roll away the stone in front of Lazarus' tomb. You protest vehemently, but Jesus insists. You tell him that this is a repulsive and offensive thing to do, but he insists again.

Hear Jesus ask some of the men to roll away the stone and see their resistance. Some of them shrink away. A few brave men move toward the stone, while others in the crowd quickly cover their faces. Some run back toward the house. You want to run too, but something in Jesus' voice makes you stay. You hear him praying, and while you don't understand his prayer, you sense that life is going to spring forth out of this despair.

*What in your own life is Christ asking you to do?*

*Is there something that seems strange,*
*that you know you are to do?*

*Perhaps Christ is even calling you*
*to do something that seems offensive to you.*

*Do you, like Martha, need to obey him?*

*Day 7*

Perhaps you are one of the friends who has come to comfort the bereaved. It doesn't matter who you are today, for the call of Christ reaches down into the recess of every heart with the same message.

"Come forth!" Jesus cries into the darkness of death. "Come forth!"

Hear that compelling plea of Jesus ring out across the stillness of the day. Hear the cry echo over and over again. As you stand before the tomb of loss, you wait in expectancy. You hold your breath, standing on tiptoe with excitement. You want to believe, but you scarcely can. Never before have you seen life restored.

Imagine your utter shock and amazement when Lazarus comes forth from the tomb. See the crowd shrink back in awe and wonder. Watch his sisters rush forward to release their brother from the binding grave clothes.

You are dumbstruck. God is alive, and he still moves. You have seen him bring Lazarus from death. What will you tell your friends?

*In your own life, you may be experiencing death.*

*You may know the death of your spirit.*

*You may be walking through the death of a relationship or the ending of a particular time in your life.*

*The giftedness within you may be dying.*

*Hear the one who gives life call to you,*
*"Come forth!"*
*Open your heart to life!*

# Stand Up!

LUKE 13:10-17

*Day 1*

The setting for this week's meditation is one of the synagogues where Jesus taught during his early ministry.

Picture the synagogue rulers seated in various places around Jesus. Here and there, a casual bystander observes the dynamics between this unusual teacher and the Jews. Jesus' closest friends, the disciples, are keenly aware of how his teaching is affecting the Pharisees and other religious officials.

Imagine yourself as a woman in their midst. Your back is completely bowed; you cannot look into anyone's face. You have been in this condition for eighteen years. Feel the pain in your back as you shuffle through the room where Jesus is.

As you get in touch with the physical state of the woman in this passage, don't miss the fact that the Scripture says she was "crippled by a spirit." Apparently, the force that crippled her spine also affected her inner self. Imagine the sense of defeat that makes it impossible for her to lift her head.

People are often weighed down with emotional burdens so heavy that the body is affected. Because a person is a whole, body, mind, and spirit all work together; what affects one part affects the others.

*What burden are you carrying?*

*Has something crippled you with its weight?*

*See yourself bowed over,*
*walking into the room where Jesus is.*

# Day 2

The woman in this week's meditation experiences an actual healing of her body and spirit. A possible application of the Scripture is to see the woman as representative of the feminine aspect in either a man or a woman. Since each human being has both masculine and feminine strengths, it is possible to identify with the woman whether you are a man or a woman.

As you move into the silence today, try to picture the feminine part of your own personality, the emotional, intuitive, and sensitive aspect. It is the part of you that is willing to be vulnerable and receptive, adaptive and open. The feminine self is cooperative and dependent, willing to yield and be self-giving.

Masculine strengths are revealed when a person is being logical, rational, and assertive. Either male or female can manifest the masculine traits of independence, dominance, and power.

In our culture that values masculine strengths more, the feminine side of an individual is often devalued or denied. Many people have been conditioned even to be ashamed of the feminine traits and do not want to reveal them.

*In this Scripture,*
*the woman can stand for*
*the feminine part of you that is crippled.*

*Ask the Living Christ to show you*
*the condition of your feminine strengths.*

# Day 3

Return to the scene in the synagogue and hear the voice of Jesus as he teaches the religious leaders. Hear their questions and see them fidget when he says something that makes them uncomfortable.

Again, imagine that you are the woman who is bent over and that you are walking through the synagogue. You are accustomed to being ignored; no one wants to relate to someone so bowed down that she can look only at the floor! Besides, you are just a woman. And so you shuffle through the room, never dreaming that anyone will notice you.

"Woman!" someone calls, but you don't think for a moment that the attention is focused on you. Again, though, that voice calls, and one of the men takes your arm, turns you around, and guides you toward the voice. Terror strikes a chord in your heart. You don't know what to expect. Surely you must have done something wrong!

"Woman," the voice says, "you are set free from your infirmities. Stand up! Be whole!"

And then he puts his hands on your aching back, and you feel it begin to straighten, one vertebra at a time.

*Can you imagine the hands of Jesus*
*placed on your pain?*

*What part of you do you need to allow Jesus*
*to lift to wholeness?*

*Is the feminine part of you*
*beaten down and bowed under the weight*
*of your masculine strengths?*

*Day 4*

Move your attention back to the synagogue, at the moment when Jesus lays his hands on the crippled woman. This time, however, place yourself in the position of the synagogue ruler.

You have been sitting on the fringes of the group gathered around Jesus. You would like to be closer to him so that you can make sure you are really hearing what he is saying. Frankly, though, you don't want to be seen too close to him; you can't afford to give that much credence to what he is doing. You have to be careful about your reputation; you don't want to lose your position or your job.

For many years this crippled woman has shuffled back and forth through the hallways and grounds where women are allowed. You never paid much attention to her; there is always some beggar or cripple hanging around the synagogue.

Now though, right before your skeptical eyes, this man Jesus calls the woman to him. If that weren't radical enough, he tells her she is set free! Who does he think he is?

Before you can recover from this, Jesus lays his hands on the woman. You watch closely as the crippled woman you have seen for years begins to stand up. Notice the look that passes between her and Jesus. See the ecstasy on her face. Hear her praising Jesus.

*Would you let Jesus heal your crippled spirit?*

# Day 5

Today, be a disciple! Use your imagination to recreate the scene of Jesus' healing the bent-over woman right in the middle of the synagogue.

Watch as she straightens to an upright position. Feel the joy bubble up in your heart as it has so many times when you have seen Jesus restore a broken body or a bruised spirit. Catch the eye of another disciple; the look that passes between you is one of understanding. How fortunate you are to be one of Jesus' good friends!

The praises of the woman are barely out of her mouth, however, before the murmur of the Jewish leaders rises to an angry roar. The vengeful and critical spirit of the synagogue official overtakes the moment, and the joyful mood is lost. The woman disappears into the crowd, and your attention is fixed on Jesus and his accusers. Your stomach tightens in a clench that is becoming too familiar.

Shouldn't Jesus be more discreet about where he performs his miracles? Shouldn't he be more careful for himself and his reputation? And while you are thinking about it, you wouldn't mind if he would consider your reputation. It isn't all that easy, being a follower of somebody who is forever in trouble with the establishment!

*As you sit in the silence,*
*ask yourself if your relationship with Jesus*
*ever makes you uncomfortable with others.*

# Day 6

You are again the ruler of the synagogue, and it is time for you to defend your faith! You stand up and speak, shaking your finger in Jesus' face. You want him to know that healing the crippled woman on the Sabbath is a violation of the law!

See yourself turn to leave the room, anger at this radical Jesus boiling in your body. Venom fairly leaps from your eyes. You must rid your synagogue of his influence.

As you leave, you are aware that you are trembling as much from what you have just seen as from anger. You have never seen someone healed right before your eyes. You pause and turn to take one more look at Jesus.

There he stands, that Jesus, like a king or a ruler! He is so poised and calm against your fury. And when he begins to speak about the law, quietly and with such authority, you are humiliated beyond anything you can ever remember. He makes such good sense!

You, a person learned in the law, have no comeback. You have no argument against the supreme confidence of Jesus.

Suddenly you feel as if you are a beginner in life, as if you really don't have all the answers. But you don't quite know how to behave without your mask of authority.

*What would happen*
*if you admitted that you didn't know it all,*
*and that your old answers didn't square with Jesus' love?*

*Day 7*

Picture yourself as one of Jesus' fickle followers. You aren't in the inner circle; instead, you are one who comes and goes, depending on what else you have to do that day. Besides, the old religious ways have a pretty tight hold on you.

Today, you are going to the synagogue to join Jesus and the disciples. Something Jesus said the last time you heard him teach piqued your curiosity, and you want to ask him some questions—if you can work up the courage.

As you approach the synagogue, you notice a commotion on the steps, and when you look more closely, you see a woman singing praises. You start to pass her by when you recognize the faded shawl of the crippled woman to whom you have tossed an occasional coin.

Can it be that she is standing upright? What has happened to her? How is it that she is moving about so freely?

Before you can take it all in, she rushes up to you and tells you her story. She says she didn't even have to approach the rabbi; he called her to him! She didn't have to ask him for healing; he took the initiative to speak the words of healing, and then he put his hands on her, and her back began to straighten.

*Ask the Spirit of Christ to release you*
*from the bondage of legalism*
*so you may rejoice in his freedom.*

# The Healing Touch

MARK 5:21-43

## Day 1

There was often a multitude following Jesus, waiting for him to teach them or clamoring for him to do another miracle. The Gospels are filled with spectators, but what really stands out are those face-to-face encounters Jesus had with certain individuals. Out of those one-on-one meetings, lives were touched at the deepest level and changed from the inside out.

There are many who wait, safely sheltered within the impersonal multitude, to observe what Christ will do to and for others. They may watch while others worship, secretly envying their apparent ease in trusting Christ. Still others may linger on the fringes of the crowd, desperately longing for someone to notice them, but deeply fearful of authentic risky involvement.

Imagine yourself as a spectator in the multitude crowded around Jesus. Perhaps you are stirred by curiosity. Perhaps you desire what you see in others, but you aren't quite sure you want to put yourself in the position of risk. Perhaps you fear becoming a "fanatic."

*Ask the Living Christ to show you how
to move out of the crowded pathways of your life
to participate in life with him.*

*Ask him to free you
from the limited point of view
of your culture.*

## Day 2

Envision the scene in this week's Scripture. See and hear the crowd pressing around Jesus; hear the boisterous voices calling out questions and pleading for healing.

As you stand in the crowd, watch one of the important leaders of the village, Jairus, moving resolutely toward Jesus. You are surprised that he is approaching Jesus, but when you notice that his face is drawn, you draw closer so that you can hear their conversation.

Listen as Jairus calls Jesus' name with an urgent, tight voice. What does the crowd do as Jairus moves through them, elbowing them out of his way? How do they respond to the anxiety in Jairus' voice?

You wonder what is so urgent that Jairus is willing to risk his reputation to come to Jesus in the midst of a crowd. You tell yourself that this must be a last-resort effort. Jairus can usually work things out or buy his way out of difficulty. He must really be in trouble to humble himself.

Notice how Jesus turns from the crowd and focuses his complete attention on Jairus. What is the expression on Jesus' face?

*As you pray today,*
*ask yourself what it would take*
*to move you to the place of risking all to come to Jesus.*

*Are you willing*
*to ask him for what you need today?*

*Day 5*

The scene in this week's meditation is interrupted by a woman with a hemorrhage. Just as Jairus is about to pour out his heart, the woman, an outcast because of her condition, comes and stands behind Jesus.

Picture yourself as that woman, standing at the fringes of the crowd, keeping a proper distance to protect yourself from the scorn of the crowd. Imagine moving through the crowd toward Jesus. What would make you willing to do that?

Feel the rush of your heartbeat as you move toward Jesus. What are you telling yourself as you reach out toward him? Does anyone in the crowd speak to you, or are they all so preoccupied with their own "stuff" that they don't bother with you? Does anyone try to keep you from touching Jesus?

As you make your move toward Jesus, be aware of your feeling of determination. You think that just touching the hem of his garment may be your last resort, and so there is a sense in which you are desperate. On the other hand, you have nothing to lose; nothing else you have tried has worked.

*In your own personal life,*
*if you are at the end of your rope, give thanks!*

*Now you know that the only thing*
*that will fill the God-shaped vacuum in your heart is God.*

*All it takes is opening your heart and reaching out to God*

*God will do the rest.*

*Are you ready?*

*Day 4*

Picture yourself again as part of the crowd that presses around Jesus. Sense the galvanizing shock when this outcast woman breaks with tradition and touches the rabbi. Hear the quiet in the air as they wait, breathless with anticipation, to see what Jesus will do.

Now imagine that you are the woman, suddenly healed because of the power that flows from Jesus. Feel twelve years of agony and pain roll off your shoulders. Imagine the freedom and lightness of health flooding into your body and coursing through your veins.

You stand there waiting for the eyes of the healer to seek you out and identify you as the one he healed. Imagine the fear of censure and the high emotion that comes with being the center of attention. Now see yourself falling at his feet and stating clearly for all to hear the whole truth about yourself.

As you kneel in the dust, prostrate and trembling, feel the gentle hands of Jesus reach down and help you to your feet. Out of the corner of your eye, see the crowd pull away from you; hear their gasps and murmurings. Do you want to run away? Do you cry? Do your knees buckle as Jesus lifts you to your feet and looks straight into your eyes?

See the healer smile at you, and feel the warmth of that smile flood you with new life. You know that his care is your cure.

*The healer wants to come to you now.*

*Will you let him?*

# *Day 5*

Return your attention to the distraught Jairus who came to Jesus on behalf of his daughter. Feel his impatience as Jesus interrupts the conversation to meet the need of the outcast woman. Surely she could have waited a little longer; after all, she is old and has had her condition for so many years!

What do you say to Jesus? What are you feeling when he doesn't stay on your agenda or timetable? You are accustomed to people following your orders. How do you feel about this man who operates on his own authority?

See a friend hurry toward you. Hear him tell you that your daughter is already dead. Feel the grief well up in you like a volcano and explode in wails of anguish. What do you do now? What do you say to Jesus?

Now see yourself as the woman who has been healed. How do you feel about your healing in light of the fact that someone else has died while you were being healed? How do you respond to the expressions on the faces around you? What do you do now? Where do you go?

*No matter how things may seem at the time,*
*Jesus knows what he is doing.*

*The task of the follower is*
*to trust him, to receive instruction from him, and to obey.*

*More than anything,*
*Jesus wants us to love him enough*
*to surrender to him the things we love the most.*

*Can you surrender your greatest treasure?*

# Day 6

Move your attention now to the person of one of the disciples as you walk along the dusty road toward the house of Jairus. Feel the anxiety knot your shoulders and stiffen your neck. You don't know whether to comfort Jairus or scream at Jesus; the tension between them engulfs you.

As you see Jairus' house, your heart sinks; the professional mourners have already gathered. With Jairus on one side and Jesus on the other, walk up to the house, through the weeping mourners. See the mother leaning on a friend; hear her cries. Feel a knot in your stomach; not only does the grief overwhelm you, but the knowledge that Jesus came too late grips you. How can you explain this to your friends who are calling him an impostor and a charlatan?

You are aghast when Jesus tells the mourners to stop their mourning. You hear the jeers and derisive laughter. Someone in the yard calls your name, but you don't look at him. You cannot bear the humiliation. Instead, you shudder. How did you get yourself into this mess, anyway? You would run away, but you can't.

Hear Jesus order the skeptics out of the house. See him move majestically and quietly into the room where the child is lying and take her by the hand. Hear him call her name. See her get up, alive and well.

*Is your life with Christ costing you something?*

*Perhaps healing will come to you*
*as you enter into the healing of others.*

*Day 7*

Today, take the part of the mother of the child who has been pronounced dead. Feel yourself leaning against a friend; imagine the unbearable grief of life without your child.

You see your husband coming toward the house with some strange men. One of them, a man they call Jesus, moves boldly into your home and enters the room where your child's body is lying.

See yourself follow Jesus. What do you feel as Jesus touches your child? What do you do? What are your fears? What are your hopes? What do you want to say to this tardy healer now that your child is dead?

Sense the breathless expectation. Every nerve in your body is raw; every muscle is tensed. Feel the dryness in your mouth. Hear the silence in the room. You are afraid to witness this encounter, but you cannot look away. You cling to your friend for support.

Watch as your child opens her eyes. See her smile at you and then rise up and walk out of this room of illness and death. See her leave the past behind. Hear Jesus ask for food for her, and then rush to prepare it for her. See her devour her food.

*Perhaps the little child in you is dead.*

*Perhaps you never were allowed to be a little child.*

*Recreate this scene with Jesus over and over, seeing the
Living Christ breathe new life into the little child in you.*

*How will the future be different for you
with this part of your personality alive and well?*

# Count the Cost

LUKE 9:57-62

## Day 1

During this week, you will identify closely with the disciples. You are part of the group that has chosen to follow Jesus. You have spent time with him, listened to his teaching, and watched him perform miracles and heal people.

At night, before you fall asleep, the events of the day with Jesus crowd into your mind. You recall the way he deals with people and the kinds of things he says to them. You ponder the way the crowds throng around him; you puzzle over the adverse reaction of the Pharisees. Sometimes you understand what he is doing and saying. At other times Jesus is a mystery your mind cannot grasp.

Imagine that you have been with Jesus in an intense period of his ministry. See yourself with the other disciples, walking along a road toward Jerusalem. Use all your senses to smell the desert fragrances, to hear the talking among the others, to see the road in front of you. Watch Jesus as he talks with your friends, looking them in the eye, taking their questions seriously, teasing them now and then.

As you walk and talk with Jesus, you carry in the back of your mind the reality of explaining this friendship to your family and friends. How do you do it?

*How does your friendship with Christ*
*fit with your human relationships?*

*Day 2*

Return to the desert pathway of yesterday, as you walk with the carpenter from Nazareth. Watch the others and see how they relate to Jesus.

In your imagination, construct a conversation between yourself and another disciple about whether or not you are going to keep following Jesus from place to place, putting yourselves in difficult positions, and yet gaining so much from your contact with him.

As you walk along, you are aware of a shift in your emotional state. All of a sudden, you know that you want to commit to Jesus with everything in you, no matter how it affects others. With that commitment, you feel yourself become strong and focused; it is as if the strength was waiting for the commitment.

See yourself move quietly to the front of the group so that you are walking beside Jesus. Watch as he turns and smiles at you. He asks you a couple of questions about your day, but he doesn't push you to be something you aren't. In Jesus' presence, you are at ease, and you feel good about who you are.

Look at Jesus and tell him that you will follow him wherever he goes. What does Jesus do? Does he stop walking, or does he continue on his pathway? Does he reach out and touch you? How does he accept your commitment to him?

*In the silence,*
*see yourself pledging yourself to Jesus.*

# Day 8

In your mind's eye, reconstruct that moment when you tell Jesus that you have decided to commit your whole life to him. As the two of you walk side by side along the dusty path, hear Jesus tell you that following him won't be easy. He offers you no tangible rewards or benefits.

Jesus doesn't draw you into his camp with empty promises or glittery illusions. He doesn't hold out wealth or unusual blessings if you are on his team. He doesn't delude you with possibilities of glory or fame, or hint at special privileges that might come with association with him.

How do you hear Jesus' straightforwardness about your new commitment? Do you want to be with him enough to follow him without any job security? Do you love him enough to trust him with the days and nights of your life? Is who he is enough to make you place yourself in his hands and let him do with you what he desires?

You walk along in silence. Jesus has told you that he doesn't even have a home to call his own. You think about your own dwelling place and your family. Somehow, as much as you love the security and the warmth of familiar faces, Jesus' life beckons you forward into the mystery of the unknown.

*As you sit in the silence,*
*ponder what it might mean for you*
*to be a serious follower of the Son of God.*

*Is it worth it?*

# Day 4

Making a decision about where you will place your first loyalty is a serious process. Choosing the object of your first love is crucial, for it determines how you will live each day.

During this week, call to mind that picture of yourself walking along the road to Jerusalem with Jesus. When you are driving to work, see yourself back on that desert road. As you carry out your daily responsibilities, recreate in your mind's eye that moment when you committed to Jesus.

Over and over, hear yourself making that statement of allegiance to Jesus. Hear the words you say. Now and then, when you are alone, say them aloud. Imagine Jesus' response to you, both in word and expression. Allow yourself to feel the emotions of that moment of commitment.

Think about all the other loyalties you have and recount what you get from them. Contrast the benefits of your other priorities with the benefits of following Jesus. How do your other pursuits compare in giving satisfaction? Does anything else in your life offer you love, joy, peace, patience, kindness, goodness, faithfulness, gentleness, and self-control?

Is there any other relationship that can give you what your friendship with Jesus offers?

*The decision to follow Christ*
*is a matter for the head, the heart, and the will.*

*Will you follow him as a disciple?*

# Day 5

Move your focus back to the scene with Jesus on the road to Jerusalem. As you walk along with him, feel the warmth of friendship and the joy of commitment. Enjoy the easy, natural flow of conversation between the two of you.

Another in your party pushes up from the rear and comes between you and Jesus. How do you react to the interruption? Do you want Jesus all to yourself? Do you resent someone breaking the spell of the moment?

Or, are you happy to share the love of Jesus, knowing even now that he has more than enough for all of you? Are you convinced that he loves each of you as if you were his only friend, and yet loves all of you the same?

Hear the other man tell Jesus that he is going to join him in his movement, but that he has just received word that his father has died. He says he will be back after the funeral.

It seems like a reasonable request to you, but Jesus doesn't accept the man's reasoning. Hear Jesus tell him that he must let the dead bury the dead. What does that mean? What does the man do?

*Perhaps there are things in your past*
*you need to release before you can fully commit to Christ.*

*Perhaps you are holding on to the past*
*and cannot accept Christ's love in the present.*

# *Day 6*

On this day you are explaining to Jesus that you will be with him just as soon as you take care of family problems back home. Hear yourself giving Jesus a perfectly plausible and acceptable reason for the delay in following him.

As you stand there on that desert road with Jesus, look into his face as he tells you that you have to let the dead bury the dead. Incredulous, you stare at him, appalled that this Jewish man would deal so lightly with important family affairs. Is this the kind of man you want to follow? Do you really feel safe with someone who demands that kind of loyalty? Who does he think he is?

The sunlight blinds you. You put your hand up to shield your eyes. The slightest wind ruffles your clothes, but you feel perspiration stream down your back. Your clothes suddenly seem tight around the neck. You want to run, but Jesus' eyes rivet you to that spot.

In the back of your mind, you remember a time when Jesus reacted strangely to the presence of his family members. What kind of man is this who would separate you from your family loyalties? What kind of person would call you to put him first?

*The Living Christ*
*doesn't call us to neglect our family members.*

*He does, however, ask that we put him first in our love.*

*Day 7*

As you assume the identity, in your imagination, of the first disciple from this week's meditation, picture yourself with Jesus as another disciple approaches. He explains to Jesus that he is going to come back, but for now, he needs to be excused to tie up some loose ends with his family.

As you watch Jesus deal with these persons who explain their reasons for delaying a commitment to him, you notice that Jesus doesn't become angry. He doesn't try to argue them into staying. He doesn't beg or become agitated.

Jesus simply tells it like it is about following him. He simply states the facts and then leaves people free to make their own decisions. And he remains so calm and loving with each person. How can Jesus be so centered? Nobody throws him off course.

You wonder, however, how Jesus can expect to gather a following big enough to make any difference if he doesn't insist that people stay with him. Yet, it seems to you that his requirements are pretty stiff.

When you hear Jesus' reference to the plow, you know what he means—that looking back will weaken your efforts. If you are going to follow him, you have to go for it; a half-hearted commitment is no commitment.

*Look Jesus in the eye.*

*Tell him what your decision is.*

# A Precious Gift

LUKE 7:36-50

# *Day 1*

You are a Pharisee, a religious leader of the people. You have been hearing about the controversial teacher, Jesus, and how he is stirring up your people.

Picture yourself in your home, greeting Jesus as he enters the door. Imagine the group of people reclining at the table. See yourself bringing Jesus into the room and introducing him to your friends. What do you say about him? How do your guests treat him?

Use your imagination to smell the aroma of food in the room. Watch the servers moving quietly among the guests, filling the wine glasses and removing some dishes and bringing others to the table. Musicians are playing in the corner of the room.

This Jesus is a threat to your belief system and to the political structure that benefits you and your family. He makes claims about himself that fly in the face of your religious practices; furthermore, he does things that a real Jew wouldn't do!

How do you feel about having someone who upsets the status quo as a guest for dinner?

*In your personal life,*
*there is a status quo,*
*a way you do things.*

*Would you bring Jesus*
*into the intimacy*
*of a meal in your home?*

*How would you feel about it?*

# Day 2

Once again, play the part of Simon the Pharisee. You have invited Jesus to your home, and even though you know you are bringing criticism on yourself, you are enjoying your guest.

Watch the other guests to see how they respond to Jesus. Notice his easy demeanor with them, even when they ask disturbing questions to challenge him. He never seems to become defensive.

You feel a little proud of yourself for having the courage to invite Jesus into your home. Now that you see how well things are going, you relax a bit. See yourself lean back and take a deep breath. It doesn't hurt your reputation to have this notorious guest in your home!

Suddenly you notice that woman slip in the side door, and your heart races. You don't want your friends to know that she has such easy access to your house, do you? You don't make eye contact with her. Perhaps if you pretend not to see her, she won't come in.

Much to your horror, the woman not only enters the room, but she moves toward your guest! You sit up straight and start to order her out of the room, but before you can gather your wits enough to do that, she stoops at Jesus' feet, weeping quietly, and begins to wipe his feet with her hair. Is it possible that she and Jesus know each other? What will your friends think now?

*How does the Spirit of Christ respond*
*to the part of you that is proud and self-righteous?*

*Day 8*

In today's meditation, you will assume the part of the "sinful woman" in the Scripture. You have heard that Jesus is attending a dinner at Simon's house, and you decide to go to the party and give Jesus a gift.

You think of the most precious thing you have, an alabaster flask of perfume, high on a shelf where it is safe. See yourself climbing up on a stool to retrieve it. Picture the expression on your face as you reach for it. Feel your hands close around the jar, and feel its weight as you bring it down. See yourself cradle the flask close to your heart.

You have been saving this perfume for a special occasion. Many times you have been tempted to use it, but no occasion seemed quite special enough. This is the time! You know it is!

See yourself carefully wrapping the jar in your shawl so that no one will see what you have. You are so intent on your mission that you are not aware of the stares and sneers as you pass through the street to Simon's house. You feel great joy that you are going to do something for Jesus.

As you approach Simon's house, you pause for only a minute. One of the servants recognizes you and then looks the other way.

*You have a gift*
*that God has written into your very being.*

*Are you willing to give it to God?*

## *Day 4*

See yourself again as the woman with the precious perfume, moving up the steps and across the porch, into the opulence of Simon's house. You know where all the hallways are; you know exactly where the guests are gathered.

As you move into the room where the men are, you cannot contain your emotions any longer. Quiet tears of joy and gladness course down your face. Relief, gratitude, and love mingle with the sorrow of your wasted years. For the first time in your life—since meeting Jesus—you know what it is like to feel clean. Now you understand mercy.

You hear Simon gasp. You know he will be unhappy with you for coming here, in front of his important guests, but what Simon doesn't know is that you aren't here for him! You want only to see Jesus. You are willing to risk Simon's censure and the reactions of the other men just to give Jesus this precious gift.

Your heart pounds so wildly, you think it may burst. For a moment, you fear what Jesus may do; but then he looks at you, and you know that you are safe. He is secure enough about who he is that he doesn't worry about his reputation; since he has forgiven you, you don't need to worry any longer about yours.

See yourself kneel before Jesus and remove the top from the flask of perfume. The aroma escapes from the jar and fills the room with sweetness.

*Will you risk everything to give Jesus your gift?*

149

# Day 5

You are the "sinful" woman, kneeling at the feet of Jesus with the precious gift of perfume. See yourself take your hair down and let it fall loose around your face. You know that letting your hair fall free in public is a sign of a sinful woman, but you have nothing else to wipe your tears from Jesus' feet.

Those tears fall freely on Jesus' feet, coming, it seems, from the depths of your soul, and cleansing you from the wasted years of sin. You weep for the hurt you have endured, for the years of humiliation, and for the new grace that now fills your heart. You weep at once tears of sorrow and of gladness.

Gently, tenderly, carefully, you wipe Jesus' feet with your hair. You pour the precious perfume into your hand and massage it into his feet. From the depths of your heart, you offer him love. You hear the voices of the men, but you are totally absorbed in caring for Jesus.

When you dare to look up slightly, you meet the eyes of Jesus. You have never been looked at in this way and have never seen such compassion or tenderness. This man is different from anyone you have ever known before.

*See Jesus look at you with the same love*
*as he did this woman.*

150

# Day 6

Move back into the persona of Simon, recreating the scene around the dinner table. Imagine again your horror when the town prostitute moves with such familiarity into your dining hall. Hear the murmuring of your friends. Watch with embarrassment as the woman begins to anoint the feet of Jesus!

Maybe Jesus isn't all he claims to be, and you are going to look really bad for getting involved with him. If he is a shyster, you'd better move fast to save your skin. After all, you are going to have to live here a long time, and he seems to be just passing through. You should have listened to your wife and left Jesus in the streets.

You decide the only way to save your own reputation is to force Jesus' hand, and you might as well use that woman to do it. Panic-stricken, you search wildly for some way to outsmart Jesus, but before you can say anything, he starts talking to you about debts and debtors and love. What is he up to?

You are only half listening to Jesus. What you want to do is get him and the woman out of your house as quickly as possible. Then you hear Jesus ask you an absurd question. He wants to know if you see the woman. You wonder if he thinks you are blind. Then Jesus turns and tells the woman that her sins are forgiven! Of all the gall!

*Thinking back on your life,*
*recall a time when your relationship with Christ*
*made you uncomfortable.*

# Day 7

Today you are a disciple. You have witnessed the entire scene at Simon's house and, frankly, you want to get out of there as quickly as possible.

It is one thing for Jesus to heal the sick on the Sabbath and to confront the teachers in the synagogue. It is one thing for him to perform miracles. Letting any woman, but particularly a woman of her reputation, come right up to him in front of Jewish leaders and perform such an intimate deed is beyond all reason! If Jesus doesn't value his own reputation, he should at least think about all of you who have given up so much to follow him.

Your heart sinks as you hear him confront Simon with one of his stories. Jesus will pay for this. And so, you tell yourself with horror, will you.

As you watch the woman, though, you forget your own embarrassment, because you see something between the woman and Jesus that you have never seen between a man and a woman before. What you see on Jesus' face is complete acceptance of the woman as a person. Written on the woman's face is dignity and self-respect.

You hear Jesus tell the woman that her sins are forgiven and that she is to go and live in peace. You feel that you have witnessed another miracle, a miracle of grace.

*In your imagination,*
*allow the healing presence of Jesus*
*to pronounce you forgiven.*

*See mercy and grace for you in his eyes.*

# Keep Your Heart

Matthew 15:1-20

# *Day 1*

Today, play the part of a Pharisee. Feel the power in being part of the leadership of your religious community. Savor the feelings of being both right and important.

You are going with a committee of important religious leaders to observe the troublemaker, Jesus. Hear the conversation among your group as you make your way to the place where Jesus and his disciples are. What kinds of things do you say to each other to justify your mission?

As you stand apart from the crowd that has gathered around Jesus, you watch him carefully. How do you feel about the way the crowd hangs on his every word? When you hear his teachings, do you want to argue with him? Does his message appeal to you?

When it is time for the meal, notice that Jesus' disciples don't carry out the cleansing ritual. Feel your horror when you observe them eating with unwashed hands. Beckon the other members of the committee and talk it over with them; perhaps this is something you can use against Jesus. After all, if he is permitting his disciples to breach this traditional practice of consecration before a meal, he is condoning their behavior! Allow yourself to feel pride in catching Jesus at fault.

*Where do you focus on the little things*
*and miss Jesus?*

## *Day 2*

Return in your imagination to the gathering of your special, self-appointed committee. See yourself standing in the circle of Pharisees, apart from the group gathered around Jesus.

"Did you see them?" one of your group demands.

"Can you believe what they are doing, and right out here for everyone to see?"

"I don't think this man is who they say he is, or he would make his disciples wash their hands. After all, that is our law! Isn't he a Jew?"

"Somebody has to do something!"

In the midst of the self-righteous buzz, you are chosen to confront Jesus. Your comrades select you to carry their message to Jesus.

Do you eagerly grasp the opportunity to face this rabble-rouser? Are you ready to confront Jesus and run him out of town? Or are you hesitant to put him on the defensive in front of so many of his admirers?

See yourself approach Jesus in confrontation. How do you look as you walk up to him? How do you get his attention? Hear your voice as you make your accusation.

See Jesus turn to meet your confrontation. Does he smile or frown? Does he touch you? How do you feel now?

*What ritual do you love more
than you love Jesus?*

# *Day 8*

Pick up today's meditation where yesterday's ended by putting yourself again in the presence of Christ.

Hear your voice registering your complaint to Jesus, and then listen as he meets your confrontation head-on. Jesus doesn't attempt to discount your concern or to evade your question. Nor does he back down.

Stand with Jesus while he talks to you about the hypocrisy of keeping rituals but neglecting the most basic acts of human kindness and responsibility. Hear him tell you that the person is more valuable than the law.

For an instant, you let yourself remember how burdensome the laws have become. Allow yourself to recall the people you have neglected while keeping your religious rituals. You recognize that the great faith of your fathers has deteriorated into obsession with minutiae. This man is speaking truth to you!

You know that you are standing at a difficult crossroad. You can continue what you have always done, straining under the load of keeping hundreds of rules and regulations; or, you can give that up and follow this man, Jesus.

Look behind and see your friends listening. They have sent you as their representative to defend the faith . . . but you aren't too sure now about that faith. Perhaps Jesus has something.

*Allow the Spirit of Christ*
*to bring to your mind the ways you have hidden*
*in religiosity and have neglected love.*

# Day 4

Move now into the position of Peter, standing as an observer of the confrontation between Jesus and the Pharisees.

You listen carefully to the dialogue between Jesus and the defender of the Jewish faith. What expressions do you see on their faces as they talk with each other? Do they speak with respect?

Do you want to interrupt the conversation with your own opinions? Would you like to help Jesus out of this mess? Do you wish he wouldn't bother with these troublemakers? Do you think he is holding his own with the religious establishment? Are you worried about your own association with Jesus? Are you frightened, or do you feel secure in your position?

Glance around you at the bystanders. See the other disciples. What are they doing during this conversation? Do you sense that they want to leave the scene or stay with Jesus?

What about the crowd? Do you feel a need to explain Jesus to the crowd? What would you say?

*In your own life,*
*what catches your attention?*

*Is it the activity of the Living Christ,*
*or the faults of men?*

*Do you feel secure in the message of the Master*
*just as it is?*

## *Day 5*

Today, see yourself as a bystander at the confrontation between Jesus and the Pharisees. You are an inquirer on the
fringes of the crowd, investigating this man Jesus.

Perhaps you haven't followed the law because you have
seen how burdensome it can be. Maybe you have been
looked down on because you didn't observe the rituals of
the faith. Somehow, the mechanical keeping of the law has
never appealed to you. Besides, you have noticed that
sometimes the keepers of the law treat others with
contempt, neglect, and scorn.

You have been trailing Jesus and his disciples, picking
up some of his teachings. It seems to you that his disciples
are different from the Pharisees, and you know they have
changed in the time they have been close to Jesus. You
aren't sure what they have, and you aren't sure what Jesus
has, but whatever it is keeps drawing you to him.

You notice that the accusations of the Pharisees don't
seem to bother Jesus. Nothing they say puts him on the
defensive, and you like that. He never raises his voice, but,
somehow, he still defeats the arguments of the legalists. His
power feels like love.

See Jesus turn and look out over the crowd. Suddenly,
his eyes meet yours. He has found you, and that's okay.

*Perhaps you, too,
have been living on the fringes
of a relationship with Christ.*

*Today he finds you.*

# Day 6

Today, you are Peter, witnessing the confrontation between Jesus and the Pharisees. Feel the relief when Jesus turns his attention back to the crowd and begins teaching them.

Soon, another disciple walks over to Jesus and whispers to him. You overhear the disciple telling Jesus how the Pharisees were offended by Jesus' words. You glance over in the direction of the retreating Pharisees and shudder. Jesus should be more careful whom he offends!

You listen to Jesus tell another one of his parables, and then you ask him to explain it. Feel your embarrassment when Jesus calls your hand about your dullness! You are beginning to see that your fear and pride keep you from understanding Jesus' simple stories.

One statement of Jesus' grabs you and turns your belief system upside down. With one short speech, Jesus turns the system of legalism inside out, declaring that the heart is the source of uncleanness! This isn't like anything you have ever heard before, and you know that understanding it will change the way you live.

Before you can recover, Jesus piles up a list of sins that emerge from the heart, and he equates what you think are little sins with the big ones! What in the world is he doing?

*Allow Christ to reveal to you what is in your heart.*

159

# *Day 7*

In the quietness of prayer, invite the Living Christ to search your heart. Ask him to show you the pride and arrogance that block your spiritual growth. Let him touch the attitudes that keep you stiff-kneed. Be still enough for him to tell you where you are resisting true repentance, thereby blocking the free flow of his mercy and grace into your heart.

In your daily routines, do you count on "being good" or "following the rules" to assure your reputation? Do you count on external behavior to make up for inward rebellion? Does your ego keep you bound in self-defeating behaviors that prevent you from accepting the love of Christ? Do you rely on religious observances to make things right between you and Christ? Or are those observances an outgrowth of your love for him?

Are you tired of playing games with God? Has the tyranny of the external become too heavy to bear? Are you neglecting to love God and others? Are you hiding in religiosity and missing the blessing of being loved by Christ?

Jesus Christ declared by his words and his life that it is the heart that matters. It is from the heart, that seat of the personality, that motivation emerges.

*Ask the Spirit of Christ*
*to cleanse your heart*
*and to fill it with his love.*

*Make a decision*
*to keep your heart in love.*

# Total Healing

MARK 8:22-26

# Day 1

When Jesus lived on earth, the miracles of healing he performed met the exact need of each person. With his infinite wisdom and sensitivity, Jesus knew exactly what method to use. He is still in the business, through the power of the Holy Spirit, of meeting individuals at their point of need.

Imagine yourself as the blind man brought by your friends into the presence of Jesus. See yourself being led by the hand. Who is taking you to Jesus? Imagine what it is like to be with Jesus but not be able to see him.

As you stand with Jesus, you become aware that you are also spiritually blind. There are parts of life you don't want to see because they make you uncomfortable. Perhaps you prefer to live in a state of denial so that you won't have to deal with unpleasant or painful memories or circumstances.

Are you in any way blind to the needs of people close to you? Do you shut your eyes to keep from seeing others' longings? As long as you pretend not to see, you don't have to move out of your comfort zone to meet the needs.

What truth might Christ want you to see? What sin might he be calling you to recognize and acknowledge, and then confess? What wonderful gift does he want you to see, and then develop?

*Can you pray,*
*"Open my eyes that I may see,"*
*with honesty?*

# Day 2

As you stand in the presence of Jesus, with the extra perception of the blind, you can sense that others are watching you. Your keen hearing picks up their whispers.

As you assume the persona of the blind man, imagine how it is to be in the presence of Christ. Do you want to run away? Are you tired enough of your spiritual and physical impediment to remain in his presence long enough for him to do what he wants to do?

As you stand there, fear seems to come from nowhere to grip you with its icy fingers. What if Jesus really won't heal you? What if he really isn't who he says he is? Worse still, what if you are the one he chooses not to heal? If he does not heal you, how will you feel about him?

Let yourself sense the fear for a moment. As long as you are in the presence of Christ, you are safe. It is okay to have feelings, even fear.

*Let your mind tell you all the things you fear.*

*Make a mental list of those things;*
*and then observe, with your mind's eye,*
*how your fears make you spiritually blind.*

*Let your heart tell you how your fear*
*has made you unable to see Christ's activity.*

*Confess your refusal to see*
*others' goodness or even your own blessings.*

*Let yourself see the truth,*
*as you stand safe and secure in the presence of Christ.*

# *Day 8*

Imagine yourself as the blind man, brought to Jesus. On this most significant day of your life, you stand before Jesus, vulnerable and open to his will.

You feel someone take you by the hand, and you realize it is Jesus. He begins to lead you down a pathway, and you follow him. Imagine what it is like to put yourself completely in the hands of this carpenter from Nazareth.

As you walk, you become aware that Jesus is leading you outside the village. Some of the crowd gathered around follow you, but soon you realize that their voices have faded and you are alone with Jesus. What does he say to you while you are together? How do you feel about this trust-walk?

Then, you hear Jesus spit, and you feel the spittle on your eyes. You stand very still; nothing like this has ever happened to you before. Jesus puts his hands on your eyelids, and you feel the warmth of his strong hands.

As you stand in the warmth of the Son of God, your whole attention is focused on his presence with you. It is as if everything else has stopped, and you know only that Jesus is with you.

*Moving your attention to your present life,*
*recall your own spiritual blindness.*

*Sometimes Jesus uses unusual circumstances*
*to bring healing.*

*What methods might he use with you?*

*Day 4*

Put yourself in the place of the blind man, half-cured. Having been touched once by Jesus' healing hands, you look out at the world with fuzzy vision, still unable to see clearly. Though you can identify people now, you see them merely as objects. You have a dim view of life, but it is better than being blind!

Are you content to remain in that half-cured state? Are you satisfied to see with limited vision just part of the picture of life? Do you feel sorry for yourself? Or, are you angry or resentful that you don't have complete healing? Do you want to turn from Jesus and run away, telling everyone that the man is a charlatan after all?

Gently, Jesus places his hands on your eyes one more time. Feel the touch of this carpenter's hands, and sense the warmth flowing onto your face, moving all the way down into your heart. As you remain in his presence, something begins to come alive in you.

You keep your eyes closed even when Jesus removes his hands. Slowly, ever so slowly, you open your eyes. You can see the world in all its brilliance and color! Looking around, you see the faces of your loved ones who have followed you. You see the suffering on a face here and the anguish on another. You had no idea that others hurt, too; years of feeling your own pain had blinded you to others' needs.

*If you stay long enough in the presence of Christ,*
*you will be healed.*

# Day 5

For today's creative silence, picture yourself as a person who is deaf and mute. Your friends are taking you to Jesus.

Along the dusty path, you feel the tug on your sleeves as your friends pull you along. You don't know where you are going, but you can see a crowd ahead; you recognize Jesus, the man from Nazareth. From within your silent world, you observe your friends' faces as they approach Jesus and tell him about you. Jesus raises his hands toward you, and you draw back. Someone behind you steadies you and pushes you toward Jesus. He places his fingers in your ears, and you squirm with that sensation. Too many have probed your ears, trying to make you hear. Besides, there is a kind of safety in not hearing.

In the quietness, ask Christ to show you your own spiritual deafness. Are you deaf by choice? Ask Jesus to let you hear the needs of your loved ones. Let the inner child within you speak the truth of your heart to you.

Allow Christ to help you hear others' sobs of grief, the rumble of discontent over injustice, or the thunder of gathering conflict. This time, hear the pain of the world, your neighbor, or your kinsman without closing off the sound.

*In the stillness,*
*ask Jesus to give you the courage*
*to hear the still small voice of the Spirit.*

*What does he say to you?*

# *Day 6*

As you return in your imagination to the scene of yesterday's meditation, you become aware that Jesus is still standing with you, and you know something important is going to happen.

Jesus places his hands in your ears, and then he spits. He touches your tongue, and you see that he is saying something, but you aren't sure what it is. All you know is that you have tried everything, and while this method may be strange, you are willing to let Jesus help you.

Suddenly, you are able to hear! You have a new sensitivity to God and to others and to your own heart. All kinds of sounds catch your attention, because you now have the receiver. How does it feel to be responsible for hearing?

Even more amazing, you can speak! Your mouth can form words and phrases and sentences now! What will you say? Will you speak words of joy and praise, telling the glories of God? Will you use your tongue to proclaim words of love and mercy, hope and peace?

*When Christ really enters a life as Master and Lord,*
*healing takes place.*

*The Great Physician applies the exact touch that is needed.*

*Relieved of your spiritual impediment,*
*will you pronounce encouragement and praise for others?*

*Are you willing to tell others how Jesus has healed you?*

*Day 7*

Imagine that you are one of the disciples who has witnessed Jesus healing the blind man and the deaf and mute man.

It has been quite a day. You have seen Jesus meet the needs of countless people. You have watched him match the method to the person over and over.

Walking back home in the twilight, you ponder the signs and wonders you have witnessed. Somehow, you almost wish you had an infirmity, so that you could experience the healing touch of Jesus' hands. It would feel pretty good to experience something as dramatic as you witnessed today; instead, you are simply observing others' healings.

Arriving at your home, you sit down on a bench in your courtyard. You need some time to process your life with Jesus. What does his healing of others mean for you? What part do you have to play in the work of Jesus?

Your life is pretty good. You don't have any big troubles. Things have gone well for most of your life. You have everything you need. What does Jesus want with you? You don't have a sensational story to tell, but there is something that keeps drawing you to him every day. What is it?

*The challenge for many is to remain faithful,*
*even in the mundane routine of an ordinary life.*

*And yet,*
*Christ is there too.*

# First Things First

## Matthew 16:21-28

# Day 1

For this entire week, you will be walking in the shoes of Simon Peter, the big fisherman. Your encounter with Jesus takes place in the presence of the other disciples. In your imagination, see your group gathered around Jesus, talking together about the events of the day. Hear the voices of the people who have become closest to you, the persons who have shared the amazing pilgrimage of following Jesus. The easy camaraderie is pleasant to you.

Look around the circle and watch Jesus as he dialogues with each one, giving his full attention. Hear the bantering among the disciples.

Then, notice how the mood changes when Jesus gets serious. He is saying things you don't want to hear. He is talking about suffering and death, and you cannot bear it! Everything in you rebels. Your stomach clenches. Your heart races. Your hands close into fists.

This isn't the kind of Messiah you want! You picture a warrior/king who will send the Romans on their way. You had hoped to share in the glory of the Messiah. What Jesus is saying doesn't fit with your image. What can he be thinking!

*Think how you have misconceived the Messiah,*
*wanting him to meet your needs and your agenda.*

*How or what do you want him to be?*

# Day 2

Return to the scene with Jesus, seeing yourself as Peter sitting with the other disciples around a campfire.

As you listen to Jesus tell what awaits him, your resistance builds into tension that stirs and boils within you until you think you will explode. You cannot accept a Messiah who will be defeated; it does not fit with the picture you have carried in your head since you were a boy.

Before you can stop yourself, your tension explodes into words, and you protest with everything in you. You stand up and reach for Jesus, holding him as if you want to protect him from the horrible things he is saying. Your voice rises; you hear yourself as if you are a stranger.

Jesus turns to you, always his gentle self, and tells you to get behind him. And then he does the unthinkable—Jesus calls you Satan. You gasp, and then you recall the time when Jesus told you about the Tempter's offers in the desert. Without knowing it, you have become the force that seeks to deter Jesus from the ways of God. Unaware of what you are saying, you have played into the hands of the evil one.

You drop your hands and hear Jesus telling you that you are not thinking God's thoughts. Filled with remorse, you sit down and begin to weep.

*Perhaps you, too,*
*have the impulsive temperament of Peter.*

*Ask Jesus to fill your mind with thoughts of God.*

# Day 3

As Peter, you feel the reproach of Jesus as you sit with the other disciples. You bury your head in your arms, wishing you could take back the hasty words you hurled at Jesus.

You look up, and when you catch his gaze, you see his forgiveness and understanding. He knows your heart is filled with love for him, and that your outburst was not only from selfish concern, but also from compassion and protection for him.

Wait! Is that sadness on his face something new? Or has it always been there? You look more closely at your friend, even as you try to take in the difficult words he is saying.

As you listen to his steady voice, you realize the Master is talking now in a different tone. His words are measured and serious. You hang on every word, sensing that this is one of the most important things Jesus has said since you met him.

"Deny yourself." What does that mean? Does it mean to say no to your self-centered, egocentric, fearful self, and yes to Jesus' way of love and acceptance? Maybe he means that every single day you must choose to say no to your own agenda and yes to his. Perhaps Jesus is telling you that the way to wholeness is to release your limited beliefs about life and begin to think his thoughts, do his deeds, and love his way.

*In the quietness,*
*allow the Spirit of Christ to reveal to you*
*what self-denial means for your life at this time.*

172

# Day 4

Imagine yourself sitting around a campfire with your friends. Look over your shoulder at the sunset; hear the breeze rustling through the trees.

As Peter, your mind is whirling as you sit near Jesus. Before you can process his statement about denying yourself, he places before you another concept that you can barely believe.

You hear Jesus talking about "taking up a cross," and you begin to wonder if you have gotten in over your head. Everything he is asking you to do is costly. You shake your head in disbelief and wonder how you can convince others to do this impossible thing.

Jesus talks about a voluntary act of self-surrender, of deliberately giving up rights to oneself. You wonder if you can do this act once and for all, but then you know that you must make the choice to live under the lordship of Christ every single day of your life.

It's clear to you now. If you are going to live the way Jesus lives, you are going to have to give up the crowd's view of success. Jesus has a different standard.

*Taking up one's cross isn't about carrying a burden.*

*It is about choosing to live a new way.*

*It is about giving yourself away.*

*What will you do with that request?*

# Day 5

At the campfire with Jesus, you lean back on your elbows. Jesus has just asked all of you to follow him. What does he think you have been doing? After all, you have given up your fishing and have left the normal ways of life to follow him around the countryside.

You look square into the face of Jesus. You know that he has never betrayed or deceived you. As you think back on all the times you have been with him, you realize that he has never hidden his demands or tried to seduce you into thinking his way was easy. All the ideas about his kingship and power have come from your desires and needs.

What is Jesus saying, you wonder, when he talks about following him? Is he talking about going from place to place with him, or about patterning your life after his? Is Jesus wanting you to stay in his shadow? Or is he calling you to a new adventure, a lifestyle of meaning and purpose and belonging?

You look into the eyes of the man who so sharply rebuked you, and all you see is love. There is something so compelling about him that no matter what the cost, you know you are going to follow him. Somehow, being in his presence makes you want to meet the conditions of discipleship.

*At this point in your life,*
*Jesus is calling you*
*to enter into the adventure of life with him.*

*What will you tell him?*

# *Day 6*

Sitting with Jesus, as Peter, you recall the things you have heard Jesus say along the way. They are beginning to make sense.

Life with him isn't about calling the shots in your own life. It is about letting him lead you wherever he wants you to go.

Life with Jesus isn't about easy blessings or special privileges. Instead, loving him means that you are to be a blessing. Jesus turns the value system of your society and your way of thinking upside down. You hope that he will be patient with you while you catch on to his way.

You hear him talking about losing your life and saving it. You think about all the times you have tried to build a hedge around your life so that you won't lose anything or be hurt. You recall the plans you have made to keep yourself safe and secure. Now Jesus is asking you to give up that mind-set and enter into a life of risk and chance.

You think about someone who has spent his energy seeking after the good life, only to come to the point of telling you that he would give it all up for peace of mind.

You remember your own efforts to coddle yourself and have your needs met, only to drown in your own self-centered loneliness.

*You look into the eyes of Jesus and know that*
*it is possible to gain everything you ever wanted*
*and miss out on the most important things.*

*What's it worth to you to surrender to him?*

# Day 7

There is a change in your thinking, there by the campfire with Jesus. The change in your head is nothing, however, compared to that in your heart. You know that when you give your life to Jesus, everything changes, and it feels so right.

Before your eyes, Jesus changes too. The longer he talks, the more authority you sense in his voice. He takes on a new kind of power, even as he is talking about giving up power. What is happening to him?

No longer is this just the carpenter from Nazareth. This Jesus isn't simply the man from Galilee, the neighbor and friend, the teacher. He is more even than the worker of miracles.

You watch him answering the questions of the other disciples as they try to sort out his message. You perceive that he is infinitely patient, but you notice the sadness written across his forehead. There is a gentler tenderness about his words to you and the others, and he touches you with such love and care.

You know that what Jesus is talking about is terribly serious. You sense that there will be a day of reckoning. You know that cowardice will guarantee spiritual death.

*In your own sacred space,*
*how will you answer the call of Christ*
*to give up rights to your life and take on his life?*

# The Cleansing

JOHN 2:12-25

# Day 1

In your mind's eye, picture yourself as the brother of Jesus. You have grown up with him, wrestled with him, and lived with him in your parents' home. You know your brother well.

Imagine how it would be to watch your brother become more and more the center of controversy. Hear yourself talking with your mother, your siblings, the neighbors about your brother's puzzling behavior. This person you have grown up with is causing all sorts of trouble, and you don't like it!

Today, you go with Jesus to Jerusalem and into the temple. With the Jewish Passover coming up, there is great activity and frivolity around the temple. As you lean against a column and close your eyes, the smell of animals and people fills your nostrils. The crowds jostle you. You hear laughing and shouting as sellers hawk their wares. You smile to yourself as you remember the festival atmosphere of your youth.

The sound of a whip slashes the air. Your eyes open wide, and everything in your body prepares for fight. The voice of your brother, Jesus, booms out as you have never heard it before; you cringe. Jesus is after the sellers and the moneychangers, chasing them with a whip. Horror grips you. Who does he think he is?

*What in your life is Jesus confronting?*

# *Day 2*

Imagine yourself as Mary, the mother of Jesus. You have come to Jerusalem with your family, and on this peaceful afternoon you are visiting with friends near the center of the city.

An uproar from the temple courts catches your ear, but you keep on talking. After all, during this time of year, all sorts of goings-on create noise and confusion. As you and your friends make your way to the temple, a woman you know comes running from the temple court, screaming and crying.

"It's your son," the woman tells you, her face twisted with rage. "He's turned over our tables and chased our animals out of the court. Can't you do anything with him? He's ruining our lives! He is a madman!"

See yourself picking up your pace and hurrying toward the temple courts. Before you reach them, you are stopped in your tracks by the sight ahead of you. There he is, your son, with a whip in his hands. He turns and looks at you, and you know that no matter what you may think of his actions, he has done what he had to do.

*Perhaps there are times*
*when the Spirit of Christ*
*has crashed into your life*
*to clear your temple of things*
*that aren't worthy of a follower of his.*

*What things need to be cast out*
*from your personal temple?*

*Day 3*

Picture yourself today as one of the disciples at the temple courts. Jesus Christ, the man with whom you have aligned yourself, has lost his temper . . . and you were there.

It all happened so fast. All of you were walking into the temple courts. You had seen the moneychangers taking advantage of the people coming to buy their sacrifices; they had been there for so many years that you took them for granted. You knew they cheated the people, and you also knew that the animal sellers preyed on those who came from faraway places to purchase animals for the sacrifices. You knew that the temple courts had become a disgrace, but what could you do about it? You learned long ago that it doesn't pay to fight the system.

But not Jesus. No. He had to go and make a scene. If you thought he was meek and mild, you had only part of the picture. Standing there in the chaos with your heart pounding wildly, you look at Jesus with new eyes. This man has something in him you've never seen before.

Do you want to run away? Are you embarrassed for Jesus? Do you want to go to Mary, standing silently in the shadows, and tell her to move to safety?

*Sometimes when Jesus comes into our lives,*
*he upends everything before he can bring peace.*

*Will you hide when he does?*

*Day 4*

See yourself again as a disciple, standing near the confusion after the wild scene in the temple courts. Look down at the debris scattered all over the area. See the animals running wildly, and their keepers trying to catch them.

There is a terrible silence as everyone waits to see who will make the next move. You look from face to face, cringing at the fury on the faces of the religious leaders. You observe that the other disciples are frozen in place, waiting to see what Jesus will do.

You want to run away. More and more, Jesus is putting himself in positions that make him look bad. You aren't sure what your friends will think, if you keep spending time with him. How will you explain to your family what has happened here today? After all, you have been seen with him enough that everyone knows that you are a disciple.

You look into Jesus' eyes, hoping for a sign that will help you know what to do next. There is a calmness mixed with might and power in those eyes. You have the sense that Jesus knows exactly what he is doing. You sense that he makes no mistakes, and so you stay there with him, eager to see what he will do next.

*When Jesus enters our lives,*
*he comes with power and love.*

*What does he want to remove from your life*
*to bring that power?*

*Day 5*

Using your creative skills to construct visual images and hear sounds, put yourself in the place of an animal seller in the courts on the day Jesus chose to purge the temple.

You have been coming to the temple courts since you were a child. For years you helped your father sell animals to the pilgrims who needed to make a sacrifice. You remember when you would watch a poor peasant reach deep into his purse for money to buy a lamb or a dove. You would look up into your father's face, wishing he wouldn't charge so much for the animal. He never relented, though, and pretty soon you took it as a challenge to see if you could get more for the animals than your father did. He would reward you with extra coins when you succeeded, and soon you forgot how it felt to bilk the pilgrims.

Now, stunned, you look around at the disarray. That man Jesus has ruined your week's income! Animals are running wildly everywhere. The coins from your table are scattered on the ground, and beggars and children are scooping them up, laughing with glee at their good fortune. You are an innocent bystander!

You walk straight up to Jesus, ready to explode with rage; but when he looks at you, you cannot say a word. In his presence, you know the truth. This is the logical consequence of all those years of cheating others. You bow your head in shame.

*What sin do you need to confess?*

*How have you cheated others?*

# Day 6

Today, play the part of a Pharisee. You love the festivities that precede the Passover Feast. Besides, the crowds always bring revenue to your town, and that makes you sleep better at night.

You are visiting with your friends, laughing and joking with them in the pleasant spring morning. You can't wait to get home for lunch; your wife makes quite a spread with all the relatives in town.

You notice a stranger entering the temple courts, and there is something about him that catches your eye. He walks with great dignity and authority, and you ask your friend who he is. He reminds you that this is Jesus, the troublemaker from Galilee. You wince.

Before you know what is happening, he snaps his whip and starts turning over all the tables. You watch in horror and rage as the temple court becomes a madhouse. Who does this man think he is?

Once he has done his damage, you charge toward him, joining the other leaders. "Prove yourself!" you demand of him. "What right do you have to do this unspeakable thing?"

*Often when the disrupting presence of Christ*
*brings the disorder necessary before he can bring peace,*
*a person questions God.*

*What are you demanding that Christ show you?*

## Day 7

Return your attention to the feelings and actions of the disciple who was with Jesus during the cleansing of the temple courts.

You had to make a choice that day, and you chose to stay with Jesus. You have to admit, though, that he makes you more nervous now than he did before that scene. You aren't quite sure what he is going to do next.

You try to talk to Jesus. You advise him to be more careful. You tell him that his reputation won't be very good if he makes people too uncomfortable. They especially won't like him if he ruins their income.

You are sitting with Jesus in the twilight, a few days after the temple incident. You can tell he is troubled, and you try once again to caution him about his behavior.

Jesus turns and looks at you in the gathering darkness, but he doesn't say a word. He doesn't defend himself, and he doesn't explain what he did. He simply looks into your eyes, and as he does, you know that he knows your every thought. You sense that he can read your heart; you know your body language is merely a printout of what is going on within you.

*As you sit in the silence with Jesus today,*
*let him tell you the truth about yourself.*

# Transformation

LUKE 9:28-36

# Day 1

Imagine that you are John, the beloved disciple of Jesus. You have spent a great deal of time with Jesus. Today he has asked you and two others to come with him up the mountain to pray.

Imagine yourself climbing the mountain trail with Jesus. Feel the tug in your calves as you climb the steep pathway; take a deep breath and inhale the fresh mountain air. The air is getting thinner toward the top, isn't it?

Look around at the short mountain grass dotted with wildflowers. Look up and see the clear sky above you. You always remember, once you have climbed the mountain, why you make the climb; the view from the top is spectacular!

Jesus leads you and your friends to a clearing. You feel privileged to be with Jesus on this intimate basis, and you wonder why he chose you for this special day. See yourself sit down with him and the others.

As you sit there in the presence of Jesus, you feel a oneness with him. There is an understanding flowing between you that words can't express. You wait, completely at peace in the silence, for Jesus to take the lead in conversation.

*The Living Christ,*
*through the power of the Holy Spirit,*
*still comes to his followers*
*and asks them to draw apart with him.*

# Day 2

Recreate the scene on the mountaintop with Jesus and two other disciples. Again, put yourself in the position of John, seated in silence with Jesus.

Sitting with Jesus, you are in perfect peace. You inhale the fresh clean air and then exhale fully. Over and over, you breathe in and out, and with each breath, you experience the ever-deepening sense of holiness and wonder. You relax so completely that you almost fall asleep; never have you known such security as in the presence of Jesus.

As you watch him, Jesus' appearance suddenly changes. His face changes, and you feel as if you are looking into the very face of God! Emanating from him is the most brilliant, beautiful white light you have ever seen!

At first you rub your eyes; you must be seeing things! You glance at the others, and you know from their expressions that they are seeing what you are.

This man Jesus, your friend, is ablaze with splendor, and without his telling you, you know that he is God. Your heart is racing; you hold your breath. This is ecstasy! You know that Jesus is who he has told you he is!

You continue to stare at him. The meaning of who he really is floods your mind, but your mind can take in only so much. The rest must be understood with your heart.

*God still reveals Himself to seekers.*

*Will you see God?*

*Day 8*

Spend a few minutes relaxing, breathing deeply. Recreate the mountaintop scene, seeing yourself again as John. Recall the moment when Jesus was changed, and remember the feelings you had as you witnessed this revelation of the glory of God.

In the deeply intense and powerful moment as you sit in the very presence of God, you recognize that this is a precious gift to you. In the revelation, you become aware that this special manifestation was after Jesus' words to you about the coming suffering.

You think of the stories Jesus has told you about his turmoil in the wilderness after his baptism, when he wrestled with the evil one. Thinking of how Jesus refused to give in to the devil's ploys for power, you wonder how that power pales in comparison to this display of God's might.

It is significant, you tell yourself, that God has waited until this moment to reveal this. He has waited to grace you with this holy gift until you have made your commitment to him. This moment is like a divine "Yes!" in response to your "yes" to Jesus.

Somehow, God's waiting until now to reveal the glory of Christ means a lot more than if he had done it while you were first acquainted with Jesus.

*Are you waiting for God to reveal Himself*
*before you commit your life to Him?*

*Day 4*

On the mountain with Jesus, you, John, are filled with amazement and wonder. This truly is worship, you tell yourself.

Your mind goes back over your religious history. You think about all the times you have gone to the temple. For years you offered sacrifices, hoping to earn God's favor. You participated in the rituals and the festivals. You tried to follow all the rules you were taught as a child.

Frankly, you had grown weary of filling in the blanks and checking off the duties of a "religious" person. Through the years the dryness of your religious duties had almost driven you to stop doing them—God seemed so far away.

Now in the presence of Jesus something changes. There is a shift in your inner state, a transformation happening inside your mind and heart, and it is all because of this moment with Christ.

When you were climbing up the mountain with Jesus, you had no idea that anything special was going to happen. You were simply responding to Jesus' request that you draw apart and spend some time with him. This gift of his presence overwhelms you.

*In the present,*
*the revelation of Christ's presence cannot be programmed*
*anymore than it could be for Peter, James, and John.*

*The important thing is to be open to the gift.*

# *Day 5*

Back on the mountaintop, let the fear and awe of being in the presence of God fill your heart. Feel your heart beating wildly. Your palms are sweaty. You move around restlessly. You are in the presence of God! You aren't sure what is expected of you.

You notice that your companions are overwhelmed as well, and that makes you feel a little better. Jesus, though, is completely calm, totally centered and fully certain of who he is and what he is about. You look to him for guidance.

Peter's suggestion to build three shelters here makes pretty good sense to you. After all, raising a place of worship where something significant has happened is the traditional thing to do. Your forefathers always built a shrine or memorial wherever they met God.

You become aware that you don't ever want to leave this holy site. What you have experienced here is so wonderful and overpowering that you cannot imagine going back down to the valley and carrying on as usual.

You want to hold on to this moment, keep it fresh in your mind and heart. If only you could stay on the mountain!

*Is there some mountaintop experience*
*you want to preserve?*

*Is there some blessing in the past*
*you keep trying to recreate?*

# Day 6

In your mind's eye, construct a picture of you and your friends and Jesus beginning your descent down the mountain after the overwhelming experience of the Transfiguration. Hear Jesus tell you that you must return to the lower places.

As you start down the pathway, look back over your shoulder at the place that only moments before was ablaze with God's glory. You pause and look more closely; you have been here so many times before, but it never appeared as it did today. Now, it's back to "normal." Or was it normal when it shone with the Light of God?

Jesus calls to you, beckoning you to follow him, and so you turn and walk slowly down the path. Your mind is filled with thoughts of what you witnessed. You know that because of what you have just seen, you can never relate to Jesus as you did before. He is more, so much more, than you ever suspected. He isn't just a normal man with special powers. He isn't just a good teacher or a great friend. Now you know that he is God. And because Jesus is God, and because you have witnessed who he is, you are different.

Walking down, you know that the mountaintop experience will change the way you live in the valley. Seeing the Light of Christ enlightens life on the plains.

*How does your worship of Christ*
*change your everyday life?*

*Day 7*

As you walk down the mountain with Jesus, use your imagination to see the colorful mountain scenery. Feel the gentle breeze. Hear a stream bubbling alongside the trail, the birds singing from a treetop perch. Feel the pull in your calves as you make the trip downward.

"Don't tell anyone what you have seen," Jesus cautions, as you walk down the path.

Aghast, you look at him in disbelief. How could you possibly go through what you experienced and not tell it? You feel as if everything in you has been turned upside down, and you aren't supposed to talk about it?

You walk on, pondering the fact that you are a different person. You can feel the change as surely as you can feel the brush of Peter's rough garment against your arm as he passes you on the narrow trail. You wonder if he, too, feels his transformation. Can he see a change in you?

You know, though, that Jesus is right. Behavior tells the truth. If what happened to you on that mountaintop was real, if it was a permanent change, people will see it; you won't have to tell them a thing. Besides, not everyone is ready to hear about the glory of God.

*As you wait in the silence,*
*ask yourself if you are willing to let Jesus change you*
*—and not tell anyone about it.*

*Are you willing*
*to live your changed life in the valley?*

# Do You Want to Get Well?

JOHN 5:1-15

# Day 1

Move back in time to Jerusalem, to a special pool said to have healing properties. Around the pool are shaded porticoes where the lame and the broken and the blind gather, waiting for the stirring of the waters. When the waters move, those who are sick and afflicted are lowered into the pool for healing.

Picture yourself as one of those infirm people, lying on your pallet in the shade of the portico. You have been brought to this same place for thirty-eight years; your spot has become quite comfortable for you.

As you lie there, you close your eyes and drift off into a half-sleep. You know there isn't any point in trying to make it to the waters when the angel stirs them; others always beat you to them. You suppose they always will.

You remember a time when you wanted so badly to get to the waters. You hated your family for not staying with you and helping you get there first. You resented those who were healed. Now, though, your infirmity is a safe haven. The familiar problem is comfortable for you. You don't try anymore to get to the water. What's the point?

*In your own life,*
*what infirmity or self-defeating habit*
*are you so accustomed to*
*that you no longer*
*even make the effort to get well?*

# Day 2

Recall the scene at the healing pool. Hear the sounds of water splashing and people calling to each other. An anguished man moans. A woman screams for relief. Then there is quiet.

Your comfortable reverie is broken by a man approaching you. He stands close to you, his shadow covering your broken body. You look up at him, and something about his eyes catches your full attention.

There is no pity here. You have long since given up being taken in by others' pity; their pity never has meant that they really cared, though you thought at one time that it did. The expression in this man's eyes is more like compassion and concern. Maybe he will help you get to the healing waters when the angel stirs them.

"Do you want to get well?" he asks, and you hardly know what to think! Why does he think you are here, lying on a mat by this pool? What a crazy question! He ought to know that anyone in your condition would want to be well!

Before you answer, something grips your heart. You know that you can't be flippant with this man. This is the moment of truth. For the first time in your life, you don't know if you really do want to be well.

*Jesus asks you the same question.*

*"Do you want to get well?"*

*What is your answer?*

*Day 3*

Recreate the scene at the pool. You are the infirm man, lying at the feet of Jesus. Today is a turning point for you. Jesus' question has pierced through your defenses, and you are laid bare.

"Do you want to get well?" he asks you again.

You cannot look at Jesus. Whatever is in his eyes makes you unable to lie to him, and you know that you aren't quite ready to get well.

Look around at the others, lying on their mats or waiting by the pool. They are your friends. If you get well, who will be your friends?

You think about all the years you have lain here and all the people who have disappointed you. Resentment fills your heart and writes its sourness on your face.

"You just can't imagine what it is like here," you tell Jesus, never looking him in the eye. "I've tried to get well. I really have tried, but nobody will help me."

On and on you drone, whining self-pity and reeling off a litany of excuses. You blame your parents and your friends. Whoever comes to mind gets a share of the blame. Your lips curl with contempt. Why would this man even question whether you want to get well?

*In the quietness of prayer,*
*ask the Physician to reveal to you*
*the crippling effects of your excuses and blaming.*

# *Day 4*

Hear your voice as you complain to Jesus about your sorry state. Imagine how it would feel to lie at the pool of Bethesda.

"Do you want to get well?" Jesus asks you.

The penetrating question cuts through your excuses and your blaming. You realize that Jesus is not going to let you off the hook by allowing you to blame others for not getting well.

You know you are at a crossroads, and you are scared. You know what it is to be sick and lame and to lie at the pool all day with others like you. You don't know what it is to be well.

What would you do without your infirmity? How would you carry the responsibility expected of well people? Being sick goes deeper than your physical infirmity; there is an inner sickness, a dependency on being inept and impotent, that has become a habit far more crippling than the physical problem. Suddenly, the thing you have longed for all these years looks pretty costly. To give up the infirmity and take on health seems an overwhelming risk. Are you up to it?

This turning point frightens you. You know that the way you answer Jesus will determine how you live the rest of your life. You look straight into his eyes. Can he back up his promises? Is he a man to be trusted?

*Imagine yourself making the choice to be whole.*

# *Day 5*

You are at a turning point beside the healing waters. Jesus is there with you in your moment of decision.

You think that Jesus may move on to heal someone else, but he stays with you. He keeps looking at you, and you feel as if he sees straight into your heart, as if he knows your every thought.

"Get up," Jesus tells you. His voice is firm and steady.

Wait! You want to plead with him for a few more minutes to think it over, but he doesn't wait. Your healing is on his timetable, and the time is now.

"Pick up your bed," Jesus challenges. "You can walk."

A holy hush descends. Look around. Everyone is watching you. Why don't they go back to their own concerns? You'd like a little privacy. You've never told anyone, but you have tried to walk before, secretly, at home, where no one could see you stumble and fall. It's a big risk to try to walk after all these years. What if you fall?

You look into Jesus' eyes. Maybe this is a risk for him too. After all, he is putting his reputation on the line.

*What is the Living Christ challenging you to do?*

# *Day 6*

In Jesus' presence, you are able to stand! As you rise to your feet, feel new life surge into your limbs, giving you strength and stability. Sense the excitement of a new beginning flooding your heart. Hear gasps of astonishment around you. Look at the face of Jesus. See his smile of approval and joy. Is that love you see?

You take one cautious step, then another, and you realize you aren't going to fall. You look down at your legs. They are no longer twisted and puny, but strong and whole.

Someone offers you your pallet, but you throw it aside. You won't be needing it any longer. Deliberately, you walk outside the portico and into the sunlight. You want to run and leap and shout for joy, but you hardly know what to do next.

You spend the day walking around the town. People stop and ask you about your healing, but you can't even tell them who healed you.

Later, walking through the temple, you see Jesus, and he pulls you aside. He cautions you about telling who he is, and then warns you to stop doing what it was that had made you sick. When the religious leaders ask you who healed you, you tell them. Only later will you remember that he asked you not to tell.

*With every healing,*
*whether spiritual, physical, emotional, relational, or mental,*
*there is the stress of change and new responsibility.*

*What will you do to stay well?*

*Day 7*

Imagine that you are still lying by the pool of Bethesda. You witnessed the scene between Jesus and the man you have known all your life. You saw him get up and walk on legs that once had been weak and twisted.

Lie back on your pallet and play the scene over and over in your mind. See again the look on Jesus' face as he approached the man. Feel anew the power that flowed from Jesus to the man.

Reaching down to rub your aching limbs, you touch an open wound. You wince when you attempt to turn over. The pain in your body doesn't compare, however, with the pain in your heart.

Why didn't Jesus come to you? Hot tears of anger and frustration pour from your eyes. Why weren't you the one he chose this time? The unfairness baffles you.

Think back over all the times Jesus has come to the pool. You have watched him move among the people, healing one person after another. Is it because he doesn't love you that he passes you by day after day? Are you unworthy? What is it about the others that made Jesus heal them?

*Perhaps there is something in your life*
*Jesus has never healed.*

*Will you become bitter,*
*or will you continue to be faithful to him,*
*trusting him with your whole life?*

# Lord, Have Mercy

MARK 10:46-52

*Day 1*

Picture yourself walking along the road toward Jerusalem with Jesus. You are a disciple, trying to control the crowd following Jesus. Somebody has to keep order!

Here and there, someone calls to Jesus. You stay close to him, your hand on his elbow, urging him on, keeping him on the road. You have seen him stop to speak to individuals over and over. If you can just get him to move quickly, he can reach Jerusalem soon, where he will have a large audience.

Outside Jericho, your entourage attracts more followers, and you are jostled by men and women wanting Jesus' attention. To take care of Jesus, you try not to let him see them; if he spends too much time with them, he won't be able to keep his crowd, and that's where he's going to have success!

"Son of David, have mercy on me!"

The shout of a beggar on the roadside pierces the air. Jesus stops in his tracks, and you tighten your grip on his arm. "You can't stop now, Jesus. This is just one beggar. In Jerusalem, you can speak to multitudes."

Jesus looks at you in disbelief and removes your hand from his arm. In that moment, you know that the crowd isn't nearly as important to Jesus as one blind beggar.

*Visualize Jesus standing before you,*
*looking directly into your eyes.*

## *Day 2*

For today's creative silence, put yourself in the place of blind Bartimaeus, sitting alongside the road near Jericho. Picture the ragged clothes on your body. Feel the crude cup in your hand; hold it out to passersby. How desperately you long to hear the clink of coins.

You hear a crowd coming and move toward the road, hoping to position yourself in the perfect spot to receive your day's alms. The crowd is chanting, "Jesus! Jesus!" and you recall the stories you have heard about the healer from Nazareth. Could you be so lucky as to get his attention?

"Jesus! Jesus!" you cry, shouting loudly so you will be heard above the roar of the crowd. People turn and command you to be quiet. Long years of anguish and pain tear at your heart and rise to your throat; your despair demands expression.

"Son of David," you shout with all your might, oblivious to the crowd. "Have mercy on me!"

Your voice rings out across the valley. Your plea for mercy, born in a heart that can see the source of healing, booms out over the voices of the crowd.

"Lord, have mercy on me!"

*In the final analysis,*
*the cry of Bartimaeus is the cry of every human heart.*

*"Lord, have mercy on me"*
*is the ultimate prayer of humility.*

# Day 8

Lord, have mercy!" A wail rings out, and you turn to find the person from whose lips it has sprung. You are a citizen of Jericho watching this entourage pass through your town with Jesus. You hope that Jesus moves on without doing too much harm.

Standing by the roadside, you study the crowd and shake your head with wonder. What do these people see in Jesus? You can't believe how they flock after him. Some of your friends have even left their jobs and families to follow him.

"Son of David, have mercy on me!" There is that shout again; only this time it is louder. You must do something to stop it.

"Bartimaeus!" you cry, rushing over to him. "Be quiet," you caution, trying to move him back to his place. You drop a coin in his cup, but he throws it indignantly across the road. You watch it roll into a ditch.

Angrily, you try to grab Bartimaeus. You have spent a good part of your life building up the image of Jericho. It doesn't help to have a blind beggar making a scene like this.

*In the silence of this moment,*
*ask yourself if you ignore*
*the wails of hurting people in your city.*

*Do you ignore the needs of those around you?*

*What about the shouting Bartimaeus within you?*

# *Day 4*

Again, you are Bartimaeus. Take a few moments to visualize the scene alongside the road near Jericho. Hear the sounds of the crowd. Feel the pushing and shoving as people try to get to Jesus. Since you cannot see, you are tossed about by the crowd. You almost lose your balance.

You cry for mercy, and the crowd turns on you, rebuking you and telling you to be still. Someone has been trying to silence you all of your life. You know your needs make others uncomfortable; you know they wish you would just slip away so they wouldn't have to deal with you day after dreary day. This time, though, you won't be silenced!

"Son of David, have mercy!" you cry at the top of your lungs, longing to be able to see if Jesus has noticed your need.

Feel the hands of those trying to shove you back to your place alongside the road. Feel your body resist them. Hear yourself calling for Jesus, no matter what the crowd thinks. Your blindness has annoyed them, but their discomfort is nothing compared to your lifelong anguish. Your condition makes them uncomfortable, but their discomfort pales in comparison to your pain at being a beggar.

*Perhaps something in your life makes others uncomfortable.*

*Perhaps your own pain makes you uncomfortable.*

*In the quietness, tell Jesus about your pain.*

# *Day 5*

As you recreate the roadside event near Jericho, recall the sounds and the sensation of being Bartimaeus, a blind man calling for Jesus.

With the sensitive hearing of the blind, you notice a shift in the mood of the crowd. You stand very still, hoping to pick up the movement of the crowd. You hear Jesus say, "Call him," and your heart beats wildly. Could he be talking about you?

"Cheer up," someone shouts in your ear. You wince. If only you could convince folks that your inability to see doesn't affect your hearing. "He wants you, beggar. Jesus is calling you. Aren't you going to go to him?"

You ignore the snickering in the crowd. You know that everyone is watching to see if you can find Jesus in your blindness. As if filled with some kind of unusual power, you throw off your cloak, jump to your feet, and charge out into the roadway. Instantly, Jesus meets you, taking you by the hand. You don't have to grope any longer!

The one reason for cheer in an encounter between a blind beggar and Jesus is that the Son of the Living God brings all the resources of his heavenly Father into every encounter.

*In the silence, hear the Son of God call you.*

*See yourself run to him.*

*Feel the hope beginning to stir in your heart.*

# *Day 6*

Imagine that you are Bartimaeus. After long years of sitting beside the road, blind and penniless, you are now standing with Jesus. Feel your heart racing with excitement; you are on tiptoe with expectation of what is going to happen to you.

Hear the silence of the crowd. Feel the press of humanity against you as others position themselves close to Jesus. Already you feel the dignity that comes in the presence of Jesus.

"What do you want me to do for you?" Jesus asks.

It's such a simple question, and you have thought about the answer long before you ever knew Jesus.

A backlog of memories of groping your way to your station has prepared you for this moment. Day after day, you have sat by the road with that pitiful cup in your hand. Year after year, you have waited, dependent on the mercy of passersby, while your deepest desire has gone unfulfilled.

You know exactly what you want. It isn't pity, and it isn't money. What you want is your sight, and so you tell Jesus, clearly and simply, exactly what you want from him.

You could have asked for less. You could have hedged, not wanting to put him on the spot or set yourself up for embarrassment. You have nothing to lose, though, and so you ask for sight.

*What specific thing do you need*
*to ask of Jesus?*

## Day 7

Return to that roadside where you are a disciple, standing beside Jesus, witnessing his encounter with Bartimaeus.

You had thought the crowd was where Jesus needed to put his attention, but he has chosen to focus on this one individual, and a beggar at that. You are mentally calculating the masses Jesus will miss and the missed opportunities for success in Jerusalem. You tap your foot impatiently, hoping Jesus will get on with his journey.

Then something between Jesus and Bartimaeus catches your attention. Jesus asks this blind man what he wants him to do for him. Jesus gives his full attention to a beggar, an attention that says, "You and your pain matter to me."

Suddenly you see with new eyes. For the first time, you see the beggar as a human being with worth and dignity. You sense Jesus' respect for this pitiful specimen of humanity, and you feel respect being born in you. There is a change in your own heart when you become aware of the aching, compelling need in the heart of Bartimaeus.

You watch the miracle of healing. You have seen Jesus heal others, but this time your own heart is healed. For the first time in your life, you can feel another's pain.

*Whose pain does Jesus want you to feel?*

# Widening the Circle

MATTHEW 15:21-28

*Day 1*

Toward the end of his ministry, Jesus went to the area of Tyre and Sidon, perhaps for a retreat from the dangerous popularity among the Jews and to spend some time with the disciples. He knew that his life was about to change dramatically, and may have wanted to prepare himself and the disciples for the coming difficulties.

Place yourself in the role of the Canaanite woman in the Scripture for this week. Imagine coming from a race long hated by the Jews. In your memory you carry stories from your ancestors of the strife between your people and the Jews.

You also have heard reports from the Jewish territories about this man Jesus who can heal the sick and exorcise demons. Your heart has been captured by the stories, and each time you look at your daughter, you ache with desire to approach Jesus with your need.

See yourself, perhaps after an episode with your demon-possessed daughter, leaving your house and making your way to Jesus. You feel you don't deserve to approach him, but you are going to do just that. See yourself walking up to Jesus, filled with expectancy, in spite of who you are.

*What makes you feel unacceptable to Jesus?*

*In the silence, tell him about it.*

# Day 2

Put yourself again in the place of the Canaanite woman, laying aside your history and the baggage that goes with it, and
making your way toward Jesus.

As you approach him, you forget that you aren't one of
his kind. Long years of dealing with your daughter's problem have broken your heart so that you come in humility,
without even a thought about what Jesus or his friends may
think of you. Love for your daughter, concern for her welfare, and a deep desire for her wholeness make you forget
yourself.

The past is behind you. All the times you have traveled
around from place to place with your daughter, looking for
an answer, don't mean a thing to you now. All the expense,
the seeking advice from sincere healers and greedy charla-
tans, doesn't matter. You know that this man Jesus has
something that could help your daughter, and there isn't a
Jew strong enough to keep you from him!

In the corner of your eye you see the looks of derision
on your kinsmen's faces as you approach the carpenter from
Galilee. You hear the complaints of Jesus' friends, but your
love for your child makes those problems small. The hope
you have is all that matters.

*Can you ignore others' resistance*
*to your meeting Jesus now?*

# *Day 8*

Within each person, the child of the past still exists. That person you used to be, before life happened to you, is still a part of your personality and longs to be acknowledged.

Use the creative silence of today to call up a picture of yourself as a child of five or six, or, even younger. Find a picture of yourself when you were a child and ponder it.

What was it like for you when you were young and dependent? Who did God create you to be? Did that child of God get to flourish and grow, nurtured in health and love? Did someone significant to you sparkle on you in those first, impressionable years?

Perhaps your little child had to go into hiding early. Maybe you were one of the ones who had to grow up too fast because of the behavior of the significant adults in your life. You may have missed your childhood altogether.

*Just as the mother in this story went to Jesus*
*on behalf of her child,*
*you, too, can go in prayer to the Living Christ*
*on behalf of your inner child.*

*Through this process of inner praying,*
*Jesus can heal your childhood wounds*
*and cause your inner child to flourish even now.*

*As an adult,*
*go back in your memory and see yourself*
*standing with Jesus with your inner child.*

*What happens?*

212

# Day 4

The Canaanite woman takes center stage again today as you enter the presence of Christ on behalf of your daughter.

See yourself walking up to the house where Jesus is staying. You stand outside and lean against the wall, looking inside at Jesus and his group. You know that if you ask permission, you will get all sorts of excuses as to why you can't see him.

See yourself walk into the room where Jesus is. Pause for a moment while your eyes adjust to the dim light. Everyone stops talking and looks in your direction, and you meet their gaze head-on. You don't really have anything to lose, do you? Besides, Jesus has come into your land.

"Son of David," you say, the words sticking in your throat. What would your father think if he knew you were speaking to his ancestral enemy with respect and deference?

"Have mercy on me," you continue. Love for your daughter and desperation spur you on. "My daughter is suffering terribly from demon possession."

You stand there, naked with vulnerability. Jesus can do with you whatever he will. You have stated your case.

*What must you overcome to bring your need to Jesus?*

*Are you willing to lay everything about your life before him?*

*See yourself standing*
*with open heart and hands before Jesus.*

## Day 5

You are the Canaanite woman, having laid bare your soul and your need before Jesus and his friends. Outside, you hear your own people murmuring, shocked that you would even enter the house of a Jew!

For what seems an eternity, Jesus sits in silence. The silence grows and thunders in your ears until you think you cannot bear it. Has he not heard you? You anticipated his sending you away in anger; you never dreamed he would respond with awesome, roaring silence.

Shall you stay with him, waiting out the silence? Would it be better to duck your head, cut your losses, and get out of there before you suffer any more humiliation? Can't Jesus see that you have staked everything on him? Is he who he has claimed to be? Or is he, as some say, the biggest fraud who ever lived?

You decide to stay. After all, what do you have to lose by waiting? The longer you stay, the more the struggle within you builds. You wrestle with yourself, demanding a patience you didn't know you had. Jesus' unwillingness to meet your need, or to even acknowledge your presence, is overwhelming. The silence of God is deafening.

*Within the silences that Jesus allows in our lives,*
*he is still there.*

*Often he is waiting to see*
*if we will stay with him even though he is silent.*

*Will you stand his silence?*

# *Day 6*

Visualize yourself in the house where Jesus is having a face-to-face encounter with a woman who doesn't deserve his time. You are his disciple, standing by Jesus through strange and puzzling days in this alien land.

In the first place, you are shocked that a woman would burst into the house and approach Jesus in such an audacious manner. Furthermore, it is appalling to you that a Canaanite woman would put herself in this awkward position. Of all the odd people you have seen with Jesus, this one takes the cake! Who does she think she is, interrupting his vacation like this?

You are sitting where you can see everything that transpires between Jesus and the woman. Back and forth your eyes move, trying to read the encounter. You have long since given up trying to tell Jesus what to do with strange people. The other disciples speak up, urging him to do whatever it takes to quiet her and avoid an embarrassing situation. You say nothing. Who knows what is the right thing to do?

You hear Jesus tell the disciples that he was sent to the lost sheep of Israel, and you think your heart is going to break. You know the pain Jesus feels in being rejected by his own people. And, yet, you know that he is always widening the circle of love. In the silence, you recall your own disowned selves.

*Bring the unacceptable parts*
*of your own life before Jesus.*

# Day 17

Move back into the persona of the Canaanite woman standing in the awesome silence before Jesus. You have made your request, only to be met by his silence, and then the noisy response of his friends. You know well their need to dismiss you; this isn't the first time someone has tried to force an easy solution to your difficult problem so that they might feel better or look good.

Now you make yourself even more vulnerable. You move closer to Jesus and kneel down. You can't believe you are doing this, and yet, something within you compels you to persist.

"Please, help me," you plead, but Jesus gives you some excuse about working only with his own people. He tosses out a remark about bread crumbs and dogs. You don't know for sure if he is insulting you, but you catch him with your quick wit.

Something changes in Jesus' expression. Is that a twinkle in his eye? He speaks the words of affirmation you have longed to hear, and you want to hold on to each one as if it were a precious jewel. Can it really be that your daughter is healed? You look into the face of Jesus, and you know that it is true.

You leave, overwhelmed with the reality that although you came to Jesus asking for a physical need to be met, he gave you something more. By going into his presence, you received faith.

*Today,*
*in Christ's presence,*
*receive his gift of faith.*

216

# Washing Feet

JOHN 13:1-17

# Day 1

Envision yourself in a dining room with Jesus and the rest of the disciples. As you recline at the low table, notice the flicker of candlelight in the semi-darkness. Pay attention to what people around you are saying.

You are Peter, taking part in this meal with Jesus and the men who have come to be your closest friends. Look around the table and into the eyes of Jesus. He seems especially pensive tonight. Study his face as he speaks quietly with James. Notice his directness with Judas. Pay attention to the respect he shows for the servants.

You finish your meal and all raise your goblets for one last cup of wine. A servant quietly removes your plates.

Close your eyes and rub your forehead with your rough hands. Countless nights of pulling in nets filled with fish have toughened your skin. Nothing, however, has toughened your heart enough to bear the things Jesus has been saying about what is ahead for him. You want to hold on to him.

Breathe deeply and savor this night. For reasons you cannot explain, you know you will never forget this meal.

*The Living Christ wants to speak to you even now.*

*Will you let him?*

# Day 2

You are Peter again, seated at the meal with your friends. Suddenly, Jesus rises and removes his outer garment. The room becomes deathly quiet as all eyes are fixed on him. What is he doing?

You can't believe your eyes! Jesus is wrapping a towel around his waist and pouring water into a basin. One of the servants rushes over and tries to take the basin, but Jesus motions him away. Notice the fear in the servant's eyes; if his master finds out that Jesus took over some of his responsibilities, the servant will be in trouble. He might even lose his job!

Quietly, and with great dignity, Jesus kneels before one disciple, then another, gently washing their feet. While you watch, everything in you rebels. Jesus is doing what only the common servants are supposed to do. Why doesn't someone stop him?

Being Peter, you want to do something. Should you rush over and take his place? Maybe you should command the disciples to refuse his servant deeds! Somebody should intervene and stop Jesus from debasing himself, but his stunning action has left everyone speechless!

*The Spirit of the Living Christ often works in mysterious, unexpected ways to reveal the true nature of God.*

*In what ways might Jesus be surprising you?*

# Day 3

You are Peter again, watching Jesus wash the feet of the disciples. You listen to the water as it splashes into the basin. You hear John and James softly weeping. Someone takes a deep breath, and here in this upper room, time almost stands still.

Now Jesus turns to you, kneeling and reaching for your feet. In horror, you pull back and ask in disbelief, "Are you going to wash my feet?" Your voice sounds strange and unfamiliar.

Imagine Jesus looking straight into your eyes, his expression one of love and mercy and acceptance. Is that a bit of sadness you haven't seen before? He says that although you don't understand now, you will later. Then he waits for your response. Always the gentleman, Jesus is.

Hear yourself telling Jesus that you won't have him washing your feet! Detect the firmness in your voice. Aren't you rather proud of yourself? Don't you want to send a message to the others that you won't allow Jesus of Nazareth to stoop to wash your feet? Is that a pompous edge in your tone?

*Jesus of Nazareth, the Son of God,*
*still comes to each of us*
*to "wash our feet" in a myriad of ways.*

*He is still serving us through others' acts of love.*

*Who has symbolically*
*washed your feet in the name of Christ?*

*How did you try to resist?*

# Day 4

Using your imagination, picture yourself as Peter, with Jesus kneeling before you. Hear yourself arguing with Jesus about whether he is going to wash your feet. Look deeply into his eyes.

You are a proud person, aren't you? You can do things for yourself—you don't need anyone to do such a menial task as washing your feet! Feel resistance welling up from deep within. Then hear Jesus' words to you and see the love and compassion on his face.

The moment stands still while Jesus waits for your decision. Hear yourself relenting, asking Jesus to wash not only your feet, but your head and hands as well. Then listen to his patient response. Jesus names the terms of his work with you.

Feel his hands on your feet. Notice his carpenter's hands gently washing your feet. He picks the towel up and tenderly blots the water. For the first time in a long time, you know what humility is. Perhaps this is the first time in your life you have really known what it was like to be humble enough to receive from someone else.

You want to weep. No, you want to cry like a baby. You want to let long-pent-up tears from your lifetime of self-sufficiency and independence burst into sobs. By this simple act Jesus has touched you at the deepest level of your heart, and you know that you will never be the same.

*Ask the Living Christ*
*to come to you today to wash your feet.*

*How will you respond?*

# Day 5

See yourself as one of the servants in the upper room. You have been busy filling plates and goblets and then removing empty platters. It is important that you do a good job; the master seems to think that this is an especially significant group of guests, and you want to please him.

After the guests have dined sufficiently, you move back into the corner of the room. You can see the guests from the vantage point of the shadowy corner, but you won't intrude on their discussion. Their mood has changed from one of warm banter to serious discussion.

You lean against the rough wall and close your eyes. It has been an exhausting day, and you long to finish your duties so you can go to bed. Feel the weariness in your body as you struggle to stay awake.

Suddenly you open your eyes and find, to your horror, that the honored guest is performing one of duties—he is washing the feet of the other guests! You spring out of the shadows and rush toward him, insisting that he give you the basin and towel. You mind is frantically struggling to re-member, but you just know that you washed the feet of the guests when they arrived.

The honored guest—they call him Jesus—motions you away, and you watch as he washes each guest's feet. What if your master sees this? This Jesus isn't like any man you have ever seen before.

*To what act of servanthood is Jesus calling you?*

# Day 6

On this day, assume the character of Judas. You, too, have shared this meal with Jesus and the other disciples in the upper room. You, too, have watched Jesus take the role of a servant and wash the disciples' feet.

As you watch Jesus' encounter with Peter, thoughts are tumbling over and over in your head. You recall the conversations you have had with the Jewish officials. You remember how you have wavered for weeks, wanting to leave Jesus' group and return to your old life, yet feeling unable to leave.

Cynicism boils up in you like poison. The stillness of the room closes in like a lethal heat wave, and you think you will suffocate. You consider running from the room, breaking out into the freedom of the night air and your own plans and schemes, but you wait, tortured and twisted, ready to explode with impatience and hatred.

What contempt you have for Jesus in this servant role! Your mind offers up sarcasm and ridicule as you see him kneeling before his friends. Doesn't he realize this is no way to build a kingdom? Can't he see that people won't respect someone who washes others' feet? What is wrong with him?

Now see Jesus kneel at your feet, Judas. It's your turn, Judas. What do you do? Will you let him wash your feet, too, Judas?

*How does the Judas in you respond?*

## Day 7

Move back into the character of Peter. You sit quietly, looking at your freshly washed feet. You think they should be different after Jesus' washing, but they look the same.

All the disciples sit in stunned silence; it seems nobody wants to move. Finally you look up and see Jesus quietly folding the towels. Nobody speaks. Now Jesus is putting on his outer garment. All eyes follow him as he returns to his place.

Hear Jesus ask if you understand what he has done. You hang your head; you wouldn't risk answering that question for anything! Nobody else says anything, and you notice that Jesus doesn't really seem to expect an answer. He knows you don't know the answer.

"Do for each other what I have done for you," Jesus tells you. "Follow my example."

You keep thinking about how some of you want the places of honor. You recall your own need to be important in Jesus' eyes, and especially in the eyes of the other disciples. The mere thought of washing each other's feet has scary implications!

You disciples are afraid to look at one another, and so you scrutinize the floor. What will it mean to follow Jesus' example? Can you still be important if you wash feet?

*Do you have the humility
to serve others within the church?*

*How does Jesus want you
to carry out his example?*

# Surrender

MATTHEW 26:36-47

# Day 1

During this week, the setting is the Garden of Gethsemane, a garden filled with gnarled olive trees. For today, see yourself as Peter.

You and the other disciples have just participated in a meal with Jesus as you have so many times before. Tonight, however, there was a different mood. There was tension in the air like electricity. Sadness hovered over your group like a dark cloud.

It was that scene with Judas that set things off; until he left, things were pretty normal. Now you are troubled by Jesus' words about your betraying him. You want to talk with him about it, but he isn't in the mood. You retreat into yourself and mull over his words, trying to understand why he said what he did.

You and the others walk toward the garden where you have been with him so many times before. He tells everyone but you and James and John to sit at the entrance of the garden, and motions for the three of you to follow him. He says that he is troubled and asks you to stay with him. His agony is almost more than you can bear.

*In the life of prayer,*
*those who are intimate with Christ*
*participate in his suffering for mankind.*

*Can you do that?*

## Day 2

Recreate the garden scene, assuming again the place of Peter. Hear the rustle of leaves beneath you as you kneel in the garden. Look above you and see the moon rising in the clear sky. Feel the evening breeze on your face.

As you look at James and John, you see that their faces are pictures of agony and confusion. You long to speak, but dare not; silence seems to be the only appropriate behavior.

You peer down the pathway and see Jesus fall to his knees in prayer. Your heart nearly breaks when you see how alone he is. Love overwhelms you as you watch him. You wish you could take away his sorrow, whatever it is, but you know that there are some things a person has to do alone.

You think about how much Jesus enjoys being with his friends. You recall the festivals and parties when Jesus had the most fun of all. You muse over how much time he has spent with all of you. Ever since you first met him, he has gone off alone to pray, but this present aloneness is like nothing you have ever seen before. You shudder in the night air and move nearer James and John.

*Each of us has to make a journey alone.*

*There are things other people cannot do.*

*But God is always present.*

*Day 8*

As Peter again, go one step farther into the Garden of Gethsemane with Jesus. If you could go with him all the way, you would see a man in a struggle for his life.

Watch Jesus as he weeps for the inevitable. See the awareness of his coming agony consume him. Hear his sobs of grief over having to leave his earthly friends who are so precious to him. Watch him reckon with the realities to which his call has led him.

You are seeing Jesus' authentic spirit. This is the Son of God, laying open his heart to the Father. You wonder if Jesus wishes he could be somebody else and not have to suffer like this.

Does Jesus believe that all has been in vain? Maybe he feels like a failure. You know he isn't because of the change in your own life, but still you wonder. You know what it is like to do your very best and still come up short. You know, too, how it feels to be misunderstood by your closest friends.

That episode with Judas slips into your mind, and you shudder, looking over your shoulder. Could *that* have caused Jesus all this agony?

One thing is certain—Jesus doesn't hide his struggles from the rest of you. Somehow, that is comforting.

*Is there a struggle going on within you today?*

# Day 4

Take a few moments to center yourself before resuming the meditation on the struggle in the Garden of Gethsemane. In reverence, return to the position of the observer near Jesus in the garden.

You hear him begin to pray and feel as if you should move away. But Jesus knows you are there; he has nothing to hide.

It amazes you how easily and naturally he prays, always calling God "Father." You notice that Jesus hasn't let his troubled spirit or his troubles build a wedge between himself and his Father. He takes his struggle to the Father as a child would take a broken toy or a wounded animal.

Jesus doesn't have to go through any rituals either, you notice. God is his constant companion; even in his agony, Jesus is on intimate terms with God.

You think about the times you have had troubles; you didn't really want to tell God about them. Perhaps you thought God was punishing you, or that God really didn't care. Most of the time, you thought you could fix them yourself. You remember the time you blamed God for that broken relationship. God could have fixed it; if only He would have.

*Just as it was for Jesus in the garden of struggle,*
*so often it is with us.*

*Fellowship with him is*
*the only adequate preparation for crisis.*

*Preparation for the inevitable tough times begins*
*in the quiet moments of communion before the crisis.*

# Day 5

Through the gift of imagination, return again to the Garden of Gethsemane. Picture the scene on that dark evening. See yourself there with Jesus in his hour of agony.

"Please let this pass from me," you hear Jesus plead, and you start to rush to him. Something—or is it someone—checks you. You sense that your friend is in the throws of a difficult decision, and he must go through it alone. With a wisdom you didn't know you had, you realize that it is not right to interfere with another's wrestlings with God, and so you retreat.

You hear Jesus repeat his plea, begging his heavenly Father for a reprieve. You wonder what is so horrible.

Jesus' struggle becomes so intense that you lean over on a large stone and cover your eyes. You think about the things you have begged God to remove or to keep from happening that God allowed anyway, and you cannot bear to see your friend up against something like that. Yet, if Jesus can bring his petitions to God, so can you.

*In the struggle with God,*
*there is the natural human will*
*and the ultimate and perfect will of God.*

*In the silence,*
*bring your struggle to God.*

*Tell God your fears;*
*let God know the things*
*you can't yet release to Him.*

# Day 6

Again with reverence, return to the Garden of Gethsemane with Jesus. Feel the hard stone beneath your head as you lean into it for strength. It's not as easy to be with Jesus in this moment as it was when he was healing the sick and performing miracles around the Sea of Galilee.

Suddenly, Jesus' agony subsides. You wait, holding your breath. There is a stillness such as you have never known. You fear for Jesus, but when you dare to look at him, you see peace flood his face. The sadness is still there, etched all over that beloved face, but now peace is mingled with it.

"No matter what I want," Jesus says, "I desire your will more. Your will be done."

The prayer of surrender coming from Jesus' lips holds you spellbound. This is no automaton you are observing, but the Word made flesh. This is no passive puppet of the Almighty, but God's Son who became like you so that he could understand you. The Son of God was able to say, "Let it be."

Jesus Christ prayed for deliverance, but in the final analysis, it was his prayer of surrender that opened the door for God's ultimate victory in his life. That prayer of surrender assumed God's lovingkindness and justice; it was the ultimate prayer of trust.

*When you are ready to give up your struggle,*
*"Your will be done"*
*is the prayer of victory.*

# Day 7

Return once again as Peter in the Garden of Gethsemane. While Jesus has been praying, you and the others have fallen asleep. Suddenly you awaken and see that Jesus is standing over you. Jesus doesn't scold you and James and John, but you can tell he is disappointed. You feel ashamed and start to make an excuse. Then you remember what Jesus said during supper about your betraying him. Is this what he meant?

"I asked you to watch and pray," Jesus says to you, with such sorrow and anguish that you are stunned. You look into his face and see that he needed you and his other companions to stay awake. Your failure pierces your heart.

You look away in shame. Surely you could have held your eyes open while Jesus was praying. Surely you could have done that much for him. Didn't it feel good, though, to escape into sleep after the emotional upheaval around the dinner table?

*As you consider your own life,*
*think about the things you fear,*
*the ways you protect yourself against*
*disease or financial disaster or the attack of a robber.*

*Do you care similarly for your soul in prayer?*

# Denying Christ

MATTHEW 26:69-75

*Day 1*

Reconstruct the scene in the Garden of Gethsemane at the time of Jesus' arrest. As Peter, you react to the arrest of Jesus by slicing off the ear of a soldier, only to be reprimanded by Jesus. You watch with amazement as Jesus restores the soldier's ear. How can he still be concerned with someone else?

From that point on, things begin to blur. You watch helplessly as the soldiers surround and seize Jesus. None of you can see him, much less help him.

Through the streets you follow the crowd, trying to catch up with Jesus. The raucous laughter and evil jeers cut you to the heart. You look around for the other disciples. Where are they? You suppose they have fled out of fear for their lives. Perhaps you should be more cautious, but you want to prove your faithfulness to Jesus.

Your thoughts are confused as you stumble through the streets. You think of all the things you should have done differently. You wish you had had a chance to say something to Jesus before he was taken away. What will become of those of you who have given up everything to follow him?

Feel fear grip your heart. Allow anger to come to your awareness. This isn't turning out as you had expected.

*Are you following Jesus from a distance?*

*Are you afraid?*

# *Day 2*

Imagine yourself today as the servant girl in the courtyard of the high priest. You are bustling around, serving the soldiers and the drifters. There is great excitement in the air, and much is expected of you.

Hear the shouting outside the gates. People are banging on the doors as if they are going to break them down. You don't know who this man Jesus really is or what crime he has committed, but you know he must have done something really awful. There hasn't been this much stir in the courts in a long time!

You watch cautiously, all the while pretending that you don't see anyone. You have learned to make yourself invisible in this court; it keeps you safe most of the time. You make sure everyone has something to drink so that you won't call attention to yourself. A girl can't be too careful.

There is a man warming himself at the fire. You study him closely. Where have you seen him before? He isn't one of the soldiers. He isn't even supposed to be in here; you hope you won't get in trouble for letting him in.

The man catches you watching him and turns away. Then it hits you. He is one of those who hangs around with Jesus; he is friends with the prisoner! You walk over to him and let him know you know who he is. Exposing him gives you a great feeling of power.

*In the silence,*
*ask Jesus to show you how you expose others.*

# Day 5

You are Peter, warming yourself at the fire in the courtyard of the high priest. You lower your head, hoping no one will recognize you. You shiver, more from fear than from the cold.

You strain to hear what is going on, but the noise of the rowdy crowd prevents you. You search wildly in your mind for a solution. Surely there is something you can do to get Jesus out of here.

If only the others had come with you. You glance around, hoping to see James or John, but you see only a servant girl. You pay no attention to her, even though she is staring at you.

"You were with the Nazarene," the girl says, hurling her words across the fire and into your heart.

You glance frantically around, pulling your cloak up around your neck and ducking your head. Maybe no one else heard. This is no time for you to give yourself away.

"I don't know what you are talking about," you tell her, while moving toward the entrance. As you huddle in the crowd, you hear her chattering to others that you know Jesus.

*As Jesus was being tried,*
*so was Peter.*

*What evidence would others have that*
*you had spent time with Jesus?*

# Day 4

It is that terrible moment in the courtyard, and you are Peter. Feel the coldness in your heart as you try to escape the questioning of the servant girl and those standing around waiting to see what is going to happen to Jesus.

All of a sudden, everything in you hurts. Panic and fear mingle with a crippling fatigue. Your mouth is dry, and your heart races. You think you will faint if you don't get out of here, and yet, you don't want to run out on Jesus.

You tell the servant girl again that you weren't with Jesus, and you think she buys your story. You tell yourself that you shouldn't let a mere girl upset you like this. What do you care if she knows you were with Jesus?

You think about telling her that once out of curiosity you went to hear him teach. Maybe she saw you there, you will tell her, but she shouldn't take that to mean you really care about him or believe anything he says. Maybe if you say that, she will leave you alone.

You shiver in the night air, trying to decide if she's worth the trouble of an explanation. You don't want to sound too defensive, or she will think you are covering up the truth.

The more you talk to yourself, the more you aren't sure what the truth is. You remember when Jesus said, "I am the Way, the Truth, and the Life," and you want to weep.

*Do you ever try to justify your belief in Christ?*

# Day 5

Visualize yourself again in the courtyard as Peter, struggling with being recognized. Recall the scene in detail, in your mind's eye, and feel the feelings of Peter as he stood there before the fire, trying to decide what to do with his relationship with Jesus.

You are beginning to suspect that all is lost; you might as well give up and go home. Defeat weighs heavy on your shoulders—you aren't accustomed to being on a losing team.

You make a move toward the gate, catching a glimpse of that servant girl whispering to some of the soldiers and pointing in your direction. Why can't she leave you alone?

Sweat pours from you, in spite of the cool night air. Again you deny ever being with Jesus. This time you speak loudly, hoping your vehemence will convince all within earshot that you are innocent of any association with Jesus.

You look from face to face, searching for a clue as to what each person is thinking. You try not to let your expression betray your feelings. Your mind leaps from one thought to another. Will your leaving proclaim the truth? If only your heart would quit pounding!

It crosses your mind that if you don't get out of here, the crowd is likely to do to you whatever it is doing to Jesus.

*Ask the Spirit of Christ to show you*
*the ways you cling to personal safety and security*
*instead of clinging to him.*

## Day 6

The scene in the courtyard of the high priest becomes even more tense as the plot around Peter's life thickens. Again, if you can bear it, place yourself in Peter's sandals on that fateful night while Jesus is being tried. You have just told the people in the courtyard not once, but twice, that you have not been with Jesus.

Before you can move from the courtyard, the men standing in the courtyard surround you and accuse you once more of being with Jesus. This time you curse, denying that you have ever known the man.

By now, you want to get as far as you can from Jesus and from this courtyard. He is a lost cause. As far as you are concerned, your association with Jesus is over. If he fails and gets himself in trouble, you don't want anything to do with him! You've got to think about yourself and your family. You have put them in enough risk already; maybe it's not too late to put things back together.

You curse again, as if the curse will add weight to your story. You want to leave, but you force yourself to stay, hoping that your staying will convince the soldiers and the servant girl that you are innocent of any association with Jesus.

*Allow the Disturber to show you*
*the ways you try to avoid really knowing Jesus*
*or how you deny him in everyday matters.*

*Ask him to give you the courage*
*to tell yourself the truth.*

*Day 7*

A curse and a denial of knowing Jesus pierce the night air in the courtyard of the high priest. You hear them ring out and shudder with revulsion. Then, in a moment of horror, you realize that those were your words and your voice.

You turn to leave, but a rooster's crow stops you dead in your tracks. With a sickening thud of awareness, you remember Jesus' prediction. The very thing you had declared you would not do, you have done, and there is no way you can take it back.

In the darkness you meet yourself. Your character flaw is out there for you to see, and you weep in despair. You would do anything to take back the words of denial, but they seem to be echoing across the land, tearing at your heart.

You hadn't counted on the hostile crowd, and you did not know how vulnerable you were to the pressure of the mob. You thought you were a man who made your own decisions and kept your own council, but this horrid deed reveals you to yourself.

You weep. Feel the hot tears of sorrow pour down your cheeks. The face of Jesus comes to mind, and you cannot bear your betrayal. You don't know if he would understand how you couldn't stand up to the questioning in the courtyard. As you got more and more afraid, you became more concerned for your own safety.

*Peter's denial is the story*
*for anyone who has ever failed.*

*The good news is that in failure,*
*there are seeds for victory.*

# Seeing with New Eyes

LUKE 24:13-35

## Day 1

In this week's meditations, you will imagine yourself as one of two disciples after the crucifixion of Jesus.

For today, imagine that you are Cleopas. See the dusty path beneath your feet as you make your way, downcast and dejected, from Jerusalem to Emmaus. With heavy hearts, you and the other disciple discuss the events of the past few days. Grief and sadness are so overwhelming that you have very little awareness of anything that is going on around you. Your confusion over what to do now that Jesus is gone permeates your conversation.

Feel the heaviness of your feet as you plod along. It takes every effort just to move. Once you walked with a light step, eager for the next adventure with Jesus. Now you dread facing the next day without him.

You wonder what you will tell your family and friends now that your life with Jesus is over. You shudder at the threat of facing their ridicule. You had banked everything on Jesus, only to watch him die a criminal's death. All is lost, you tell each other. Jesus is gone, and you feel hopeless and helpless.

*Perhaps you, too, have come to times and places*
*in your life when it seemed all was lost.*

*Perhaps you have risked everything you have to follow Jesus,*
*and everything you have done has failed.*

*In the silence,*
*recall that sense of hopelessness.*

## Day 2

Recall the scene along the dusty road to Emmaus. What time of day was it? What was the weather like? What clothes were you wearing?

Today, assume the part of the other disciple, walking with Cleopas and discussing your profound loss. Again, get in touch with your feelings of hopelessness and help-lessness.

In your grief-stricken state, you aren't aware of much that is going on around you, but you do notice a stranger approaching the two of you on the road. You are only vaguely aware that he is with you. You don't know where he came from or who he is; he just suddenly appeared. You don't even know why he would want to be with the two of you; you aren't exactly the most enjoyable company right now.

"What are you talking about?" the stranger asks, startling you out of your grief. You are stunned that an event that has turned your life upside down has escaped anyone! Where has this man been?

You look at Cleopas in wonderment, then again at the stranger. Do you want to expose your grief to him?

*The Living Christ is always present to his children,*
*at any time and in any place.*

*In the silence,*
*ask him to make you aware of his presence.*

*Do you dare make yourself*
*vulnerable enough to see him?*

# Day 3

As you continue on the road to Emmaus, you are stopped in your tracks by a stranger who doesn't seem to have a clue that Jesus has been crucified. Maybe he doesn't even know who Jesus is.

Return to the role of Cleopas. Noticing that your friend can't compose himself enough to respond to the stranger's question, you, out of a desire not to be rude, ask the stranger if perhaps he hasn't heard about the goings-on in Jerusalem. The stranger appears not to know, and so you and your friend begin to tell him about Jesus of Nazareth.

The stranger responds that you are foolish and slow of heart to believe all the prophets have told you. His words jar you out of your mournful fog. When he goes on to tell you all about the Scriptures concerning Jesus, you are spellbound.

Who is this stranger that knows so much about Jesus? Is he telling you all of this to get your mind off your suffering? If he knows so much, why wasn't he aware of the events in Jerusalem?

There are times when the Spirit of Christ is all around us, communicating to us in specific ways, and yet we have neither the ears to hear nor the eyes to see. We are often so blinded by our own concerns that we cannot recognize the presence of Christ.

*Ask the Living Christ*
*to make you so sensitive to his presence*
*that you can see where he is working*
*and what he wants you to do.*

# *Day 4*

Move back into the position of the unnamed disciple on the Emmaus Road. You are walking along with Cleopas and this stranger who seems to know so much.

You listen halfheartedly to the stranger as he speaks. You aren't too interested in what he has to say. Those sad events in Jerusalem consume you, and nothing else matters very much.

Without even realizing it, you get caught up in this stranger's words. He is more learned than anyone you have ever known. Soon your grief subsides; in hearing about Jesus, you remember why you loved him so.

As you approach the village, the stranger acts as if he is going farther, but you don't want him to leave you. Somehow his presence makes a difference, and you want to spend more time with him. You want to hear more from someone so knowledgeable about Jesus.

When you and Cleopas ask him to stay with you for the night, he doesn't hesitate but comes right with you into the house where you are staying.

*Jesus came to earth in human form*
*and dwelled among people,*
*living and loving other human beings,*
*and making a place for himself in his community.*

*He comes now,*
*through the power of the Holy Spirit,*
*to dwell with his children.*

*Will you let him join you*
*on your journey through life?*

## *Day 5*

See yourself as Cleopas, at a table with the other disciple and the stranger you have met along the road. As you ease yourself down to the low table, you are aware of your great fatigue; but the physical tiredness is nothing compared with your emotional exhaustion.

Lean back on your elbow. Rub your weary eyes with your hand. Massage your aching neck. Sitting down at the table triggers flashbacks of precious times you shared with Jesus at the tables of friendship. Memories flood your mind, and you want to weep.

You know that the other disciple shares those memories. You hear a sob escape from his lips. It helps to have someone who shares your loss. You want to comfort your friend, but out of respect for the stranger, you restrain yourself.

The stranger picks up the bread. You think it is unusual for a guest to be so assertive and to take charge at a meal in another person's home! The stranger, clearly oblivious to your customs, begins to give thanks, and there is something about his prayer that sounds vaguely familiar.

Your eyes fly open. It is Jesus! But, just as you recognize him, he is gone. You look at the other disciple; he, too, knows.

*Where might Jesus be revealing himself to you?*

*Ask him to open your eyes so that you can see him.*

# Day 6

Jesus has just broken the bread and revealed himself to you. Today, as the other disciple, recall your feelings as you sit in stunned recognition with Cleopas.

"That was Jesus!" you whisper, and then you say it again with force, "That was Jesus!" Cleopas is silent, a look of awe and reverence on his face.

"I knew there was something about him the minute I saw him," you say. "There was something about him that touched my heart, but I didn't really see it until just this minute."

"You're right," Cleopas responds, more cautiously. "Why didn't we recognize him immediately? Why didn't he tell us who he was from the beginning?"

Your heart still burns within you, burns with the fire of recognition. The flame of love, first fanned into being by sharing those years with Jesus, is now blazing in your heart. The warmth of Jesus' love and the fire of his presence fill your mind with possibilities. Being in his presence has given you an energy and inspiration you didn't know possible. This is what life is supposed to be! What if you had missed it?

*Jesus' presence fills a person with the radiance of life.*

*Are you open to becoming fire?*

*Day 7*

Return again, as Cleopas, to the table scene in Emmaus. It is at the moment of recognizing Jesus that you begin today's meditation.

Inflamed with his love, you and the other disciple get up, ready to return to Jerusalem. Who cares how tired you were only moments before? What does it matter that it is late in the day? You don't even stop to think about whether or not you can find the other disciples. All you know is that the reality of the resurrected presence has fired you with new life and energy. Nothing matters except getting to Jerusalem and telling them all about your encounter with the Living Christ.

Feel your excitement as you make the journey back to Jerusalem. It seems your feet are hardly touching the road. Imagine the joy you feel at discovering the eleven disciples huddled together in a closed room. See yourself banging on the door, demanding entrance. Imagine their startled faces.

"It is true!" you shout, moving from one to the other, embracing each one. "He is alive! Jesus has risen! He has come back to us, and we have seen him!"

Sitting down with the others, calm yourself so they can understand you. Tell them every detail of your experience with Jesus.

*There are those who long to know that Jesus is alive.*

*Will you tell them?*

# My Lord and My God

JOHN 20:24-31

*Day 1*

If you had been one of the disciples, would you be Thomas? Would you be the skeptic among the group, demanding proof and standing firm in your insistence to see for yourself?

Imagine that you are Thomas in those eventful days after the crucifixion. You have been with Jesus and have watched him throughout his life on this earth. After he died, you were thankful for the time you had with him but were also realistic enough to know you needed to move on to other things.

See yourself talking with the disciples on a bright morning after the crucifixion. You have been trying to put your life back together and make up for the time you have been away from your own concerns. The other disciples have sought you out and are whispering outlandish things.

"He has come back," they tell you. You try to ignore them, but they are persistent. Can't they see you don't want to play games about something that affected you as much as your life with Jesus?

"The Lord has risen, Thomas, just as he said he would," they insist.

"How do you know?" you ask.

"We have seen him!"

Now, what will you do?

*Ask Jesus to reveal to you*
*your own skepticism and cynicism.*

## *Day 2*

You are Thomas again. It has been a week since the disciples told you about Jesus coming to them. You have tried to get those thoughts out of your mind—you can't bear to stir up false hopes. The mere possibility that the disciples might be telling the truth burns in your mind and heart, inflaming you with an optimism that is totally out of character for you.

The others send word that they will be gathering again tonight and want you to join them. First you say yes, then you say no. It isn't like you to be so wishy-washy. Usually you know what you want and don't waver back and forth. You want to believe that what they have said is true, but this time you just aren't sure.

Finally you pull away from your family, but you don't tell them why you are going to the gathering; they might think you had lost your mind. Besides, it wouldn't be fair to raise false hope for them.

You recall the words you said to the other disciples about what it would take for you to believe. Somehow it made you feel stronger and more in control to name your terms for believing that Jesus really had come back. There was some power in holding your ground, yet letting them know that Jesus had to meet you on your terms now. After all, you had given up a lot for him.

*What are your terms*
*for believing in the Living Christ?*

# Day 3

Feel the door handle in your hand, Thomas. Pause for a moment and caress the rough wood of the door, buying time before you go into the room with the disciples. Look above you at the stars in the clear sky. Take a deep breath and let the night air fill your lungs. Tell yourself once more that what they have said about Jesus being alive probably isn't true.

Walk into the room, Thomas, and hear their greetings. Do they have to make such a big deal about your coming? Do they have to hug you? Don't they know that the fellowship is forever changed now that Jesus has left you?

Turn around, Thomas, and lock the door behind you. Use your agile hands to lift the metal bolt and slip it into place. Be sure that you make it hard for Jesus to get in.

Look in front of you, Thomas. It is Jesus! How did he get in? He wasn't there when you entered, and there is only one door, which you locked carefully. Rub your eyes. Maybe it isn't really Jesus. The light is pretty dim.

Look at Jesus, Thomas. As he says, "Peace be with you," your heart races. It is Jesus!

"Put your hand here, Thomas," Jesus says. "Feel my wounds. And then stop doubting and believe."

What will you do now, Thomas? The Master has met you at the point of your need. He has met you in your doubt.

*Do you trust Jesus to meet you in your doubts?*

# *Day 4*

Reconstruct that moment, Thomas, when Jesus rivets your attention to his wounds. Hear everyone in the room stop talking to wait in holy silence and to watch this encounter between you and Jesus.

Stand face to face with Jesus, your eyes caught by the fire of love in his face. This is the moment you have anticipated all of your life, the moment of transformation you knew was possible, though you didn't know how or why. Suddenly you know that it is the *who* that makes the *how* and *why* insignificant.

"Feel my wounds, Thomas," Jesus tells you.

You look at the wounds, and great gulfs of grief wash over you until you think you will faint. Jesus reaches out to steady you, and you remember the waves he stilled and the fear he dispelled.

Slowly you reach out and touch the wound in Jesus' side. You take his hands and feel the prints of the nails. You look into his eyes and see his broken heart with the vision of a believer. And you weep tears of joy at being set free from the prison of your cynicism. You cry unashamedly with the ecstasy of belief.

*In the silence,*
*recall the horror of Jesus' wounds.*

*Remind yourself that those wounds are for you.*

*Jesus' broken body and spilled blood were allowed*
*by his Father so that you might know eternal life*
*. . . so that you might be inflamed with his love.*

# Day 5

You are Thomas again, at that great moment of moving from darkness into light. Jesus Christ, the Son of the Living God, has honored you by accommodating himself to your need. Jesus Christ,God—has revealed himself to you in specific ways you can understand.

You are now aware of the others in the room. You hear their breathing, the room is so still. Here and there you detect a sob, and you want to shout at the top of your lungs, "He is risen! Jesus is risen indeed!"

In the moment of that encounter between you and Jesus, you have spanned great gulfs. You don't have to hide your doubts from him; he understands them! You don't have to pretend that you believe when you don't; Jesus can tell the difference between honest doubt and sanctimonious pretense. You don't have to put your mind with its intellectual wonderings in a box and try to stop thinking; the Lord of life who created your mind wants you to use it. There isn't any question too big for Jesus; and there isn't any question that will scare him away from you.

*Perhaps there is some big question about Jesus*
*that has haunted you for years,*
*that blocks you from a full, vital love relationship with him.*

*He has an answer for that question.*

*The answer starts with his presence.*

# Day 6

Again, picture yourself as Thomas, just after your encounter with Jesus. Sense the joy of new life in your heart. Feel the burning of his love, warming and inspiring you with new energy and enthusiasm.

Turn and look at each face. Now, with the eyes of Christ watching, you view the others differently. You see their familiar faces through the eyes of love. You are filled with compassion for them and a deep oneness. That isn't usual for you, but you like the way it feels.

During the next few days, you stay with Jesus and the others, and it is as though you are seeing Jesus with new eyes. You watch him perform the same miracles you saw before, but now his miracles have new meaning. You observe the way he deals with people, setting them free from the prisons of their lives, and you know that this is what you are to do. You watch Jesus carefully, catching the flame of love that emanates from his eyes, his hands, his body.

In the presence of Christ, you grow in assurance and joy. This new way of life, believing, is a lot better than the old way.

*In the presence of Christ,*
*day by day and moment by moment,*
*you, too, will grow in assurance and joy.*

*With Jesus,*
*you will become totally fire,*
*filled with power and love.*

# Day 17

Imagine what it must have been like for Thomas a year after his encounter with Jesus. Think about the changes that must have taken place in his life, as he lived out the love of Christ day by day.

Imagine yourself as a doubter, as one who stayed on the fringes when Jesus was in town. Like Thomas, you had questioned everything Jesus did. Unlike Thomas, you never did get close enough to Jesus to know for yourself whether he was who he said he was.

Over this past year, you have watched the changes in Thomas. He isn't the man he used to be. The two of you used to have good times throwing darts at other people's religion. Your friend is different now.

See yourself sitting with Thomas in his home. Hesitantly, gropingly, you tell Thomas he isn't the person he used to be. Tell him you know that his change came about after he was with Jesus. Ask him if it is too late for you, even though Jesus is no longer here.

Thomas begins to tell you about Jesus and how you can know him, even though you didn't want to be with him before. He tells you that it is never too late for the serious seeker. While Thomas talks to you, his face burns with a light and a fire you never saw before.

*Do you know someone*
*who needs to hear about the love of Jesus?*

# The Question

JOHN 21

# Day 1

Once again, play the part of Peter, the big fisherman. Imagine yourself on a fishing trip with the other disciples on the Sea of Galilee. You fish all night and catch nothing.

Toward morning you are weary and discouraged as you start toward the shore. While you are rowing, you see a man standing at the water's edge. He calls to you, asking if you caught any fish. That's not the kind of question you want to hear after a night like you have had.

He tells you to put your net on the other side of the boat. That request triggers memories of another big catch, and a lump forms in your throat. You don't have time to grieve, though, for the net fills with fish, and you have to help the others haul in the catch.

John, hanging over the boat trying to control the net, looks at the man on the shore, and then he turns to you. "It is the Lord!" he says.

Without thinking, you jump out of the boat and swim through the water toward Jesus. This time you won't wait to come to him!

*Are you ready to obey Jesus,*
*even if it means leaving your boat of security?*

# *Day 2*

Resume your creative silence where you left off yesterday, seeing yourself as Peter thrashing through the water toward Jesus.

Hear the shouts of joy from the others as they, too, realize it is Jesus. As you help your friends bring in the catch, you marvel that the net isn't torn.

Stand back and watch as Jesus prepares breakfast for you. How carefully he has built the fire. He has brought bread for you too. How like Jesus to take care of everything so well. Your eyes sting as you remember that night he washed your feet.

Hear the gentle teasing during the meal. Watch as Jesus serves, making sure that everyone is part of the circle around the fire. Lie back on your elbows and watch the morning sun fill the sky with a fire that pales in comparison to the splendor of Jesus' presence.

Jesus turns to you, and your heart races. You wonder if he is going to talk to you about that hideous night when you failed him so miserably. You make yourself meet his gaze.

He calls you by your full name and then asks you the strange question—one you hadn't thought of.

"Do you love me?" Jesus asks, and you know this is a test.

*See the penetrating eyes of Jesus as he asks you,*
*"Do you love me?"*

*What do you do?*

259

# *Day 8*

Return to the breakfast on the beach. Imagine yourself as Peter. This is the moment of truth, the moment of commitment. See the reflection of the campfire in Jesus' eyes—eyes that see clear through to your heart. You know Jesus is ready to forgive you for your terrible failure. You know he is giving you another chance.

"You know that I love you," you tell him, hoping against hope that he will believe you.

"Then feed my lambs," Jesus says. You look at him with puzzlement, and so he speaks again.

"Simon, son of John, do you truly love me?" Jesus asks, peering even more intently into your face.

You remember the three questions around that fire in the courtyard of the high priest. You want Jesus to know how much you love him, and you tell him again that you do.

Jesus tells you to take care of his sheep, and you wonder why he is talking about sheep and lambs instead of about the night of your betrayal. Is he going to let that go without mentioning it?

*How serious are you about following Jesus?*

*How much do you really love him?*

*How do you show that you love him?*

# *Day 4*

Hear the crackling of the fire as someone throws another log on it. Watch the flames dance higher and sparks pepper the air around it.

You wonder if the others can hear the question Jesus keeps asking you. You dare not move your eyes from his face. This is your moment of truth, and if ever you were serious about anything, this is it. In spite of your impulsive actions in the past, you want to be firm and sure in your love for Jesus. And you don't want to relive your failure in front of all the others; it was bad enough the first time around!

"Simon, son of John, do you love me?" Jesus asks you again.

You drop your head. Three questions. Three denials. Jesus' three days in the tomb. The events of the past weeks overwhelm you, but you stifle your tears. You look straight into that beloved face and meet those tender, searching eyes straight on; and when you do, you know that Jesus wants your love more than anything.

"Yes, Lord, you know that I love you," you tell him, and you know that from this point on, there is no turning back. You are committed to Jesus with all your heart. Nothing else matters if this is settled.

*In the silence,*
*tell the Lord how much you love him.*

*Tell him you love him without reserve.*

*What does he say to you?*

# Day 5

Imagine yourself as Peter, knowing that you have been absolved of your guilt. Your sin of betrayal has been removed. You don't have to hang your head in shame any longer, nor do you have to punish yourself. You have made a commitment that will change the course of history for you and for many others.

Jesus smiles at you. and that smile is like a benediction, a blessing washing over you like cleansing water. You know that you are standing on the brink of a new phase of your life. As never before, you feel fully alive and filled with joy and peace and love. It is as if the fire of his love has ignited your heart.

You breathe in the cool morning air, filling your lungs completely, and then you exhale, breathing out anything that would hamper this moment with Jesus.

You listen carefully to what Jesus is saying, as if it were the most important message in the world. Unshackled by the past, and confident about the future, you savor this moment in the present with Jesus.

*Being with Jesus in the present moment*
*is the way to receive his blessing.*

*Being with him at each moment,*
*turning your attention and your heart toward him,*
*is the way to receive his guidance.*

*Staying with Jesus is the way to become totally fire.*

# Day 6

During your quiet time today, imagine yourself as Peter. Allow yourself to savor again the liberating presence of Jesus. Feel the ecstasy of being forgiven and restored into full relationship with him.

You ponder the charge Jesus has given you about tending his lambs and feeding his sheep. You don't know what all that means, but you have the feeling that you will know, day by day, as long as you follow Jesus wherever he wants you to go. After all, he is the great teacher.

As you and Jesus walk away from the fire, he continues to talk to you about the coming days. For the first time in your life you have a mission. Jesus has something important for you to do.

Someone steps on a twig, and the sound startles you. Your senses have never been so keenly tuned to what is going on around you. You turn around and see John following the two of you, and you don't like this invasion of privacy.

"What about him, Jesus?" you ask, and you have to admit you are a little relieved to shift the intensity of Jesus' focus in another direction.

"What is that to you, Peter?" Jesus chastens you. "Mind your own business and follow me."

*Is there another human*
*whose business you are allowing*
*to divert your attention*
*from your own mission with Jesus?*

263

*Day 7*

Take the scene one step further. Imagine yourself as Peter, the day after the picnic on the beach. You have gone back to your fishing, out in your boat on the Sea of Galilee.

You are going through all the motions of your day's work, but your mind is fixed on yesterday's conversation with Jesus. Again and again you pull in the nets filled with fish, but you keep thinking about that "yes" you gave Jesus.

"Yes," you told him, and you meant it with all your heart. You meant that you loved him enough to do whatever he might ask you to do. Now you are wondering what that means on a day-to-day basis.

"Yes," you said to him, fully committing yourself to Jesus as you looked into those compelling eyes and as he peered deep into yours. You agreed to go along with his agenda for your life. You sit back in the boat and ask yourself what that means.

"Yes," you said to Jesus, "I'll follow you." And now it is a new day, and you are ready to follow. Does that mean you must leave your fishing boat? Is he going to give you specific instructions? What will you do when you get tired of tending lambs and feeding sheep? And where are those lambs and sheep he wants you to tend?

*Following Jesus is an adventure into the fire.*

*Will you go?*

# Afterword

In the Old Testament, Almighty God walked and talked with His first children in the Garden of Eden, giving us a picture of the kind of relationship he wanted to have with man and woman. Throughout the history of the Hebrew people, God came to His children in various ways, making Himself known to them and seeking friendship. God was not a faraway, disinterested deity, but a loving Father, deeply interested in the welfare of His creation and passionately devoted to their goings-on.

When people couldn't "get it," that is, when people couldn't understand who God was, God came in human form in the person of the historical Jesus. Jesus walked and talked with the people of a small part of the world, giving them the best picture of God they could have. In the most effective way God could, God showed people, through Jesus Christ, the kind of relationship He wanted to have with His children.

In being present with people, Jesus showed that the faraway God had come near, that God wanted to be with them in an intimate and dynamic way. In making love visible, God revealed His true nature in the form of a human being.

Before Jesus left his earthly life, he talked to the disciples a great deal about friendship. Instead of giving them long lists of things to do or standards to meet, he talked in terms of "abiding in him" and "being with him."

Jesus told the disciples that they were his friends, and that it would be possible for them to be as "one with him." He also told them that he would come to them in an unusual way that transcended time and space, to be their Helper, Teacher, Counselor, and Friend. The disciples could not understand then, and some of us cannot understand now; but the Lord of Life wanted to partner with them, and he wants to partner with us, giving himself to us so that we might give ourselves to others.

It was important to Jesus that his disciples form relationships with each other, loving each other in his name. He said that he wanted others to say of his disciples, "See, how they love one another!" Jesus modeled a life that gave dignity and worth to persons and relationships, and he wanted his purpose to be manifested through fellowship with each other.

Through the power of the Holy Spirit, Jesus Christ comes to us today, revealing himself in specific ways to those who have eyes to see and ears to hear his coming. He longs for friendship with those who love him and call him Savior and Lord. Jesus Christ wants to abide with the individual believer, releasing the fire of his love through the believer and through the church out into a world that is literally dying for his light and love.

We call him "Emmanuel," God-with-us. Part of what it means that Jesus is immanent is that he reveals himself in the common, ordinary stuff of life, transforming the moment with new meaning and high purpose. God is with us, all the time and in every circumstance. The challenge is to open up to that presence; to believe is to see.

Through the transforming power of Christ's love, manifested in those who catch the fire of his love, the world too can be changed. God wants us to share the splendor of his grace and mercy and power with a world that is lost and lonely and afraid. He wants us to incarnate Christ for others; that is, he wants us to express the nature of Christ in our relationships with other human beings.

Though the meditations in this book, you have had an opportunity to abide with Jesus through the power of your imagination. You have taken on the roles of various characters in the encounters Jesus had with people during his earthly life. Hopefully, these encounters have expanded your own understanding of yourself and of other people. More important, it is to be hoped that you came to know the loving Christ more intimately.

Perhaps you were disturbed by some of the encounters. Maybe you learned something about yourself that you had not known before. It may be that you found inner healing and inspiration as you allowed the stories in the Scriptures to become your story; you may have experienced the transformation that takes place by simply being in the presence of Jesus.

Hopefully, the awareness of the presence of Christ is more real to you. Perhaps the love of Christ and his purpose for you are more real to you. You may have experienced the flame of faith building as you allowed the Sovereign God to draw near.

If that flame of love has been fanned, what will you do about it? The same piercing question that Jesus asked Peter at the beachfront breakfast reaches you, "Do you love me?"

How you answer determines everything.